TYNE
AND
WEIRD

First published 2020

The History Press
97 St George's Place, Cheltenham,
Gloucestershire, GL50 3QB
www.thehistorypress.co.uk

British Library Cataloguing in Publication Data.
A catalogue record for this book is available from the British Library.

ISBN 978 0 7509 9250 3

Typesetting and origination by The History Press
Printed in Great Britain by TJ Books Limited, Padstow, Cornwall.

TYNE AND WEIRD

ROB KILBURN

ILLUSTRATED BY DAN UNDERWOOD

The History Press

I would like to thank my grandparents Bill and Rachel Horabin, who throughout my life have shown unconditional love and support for every project into which I have dipped my toe. My parents, Rachel and Steven Kilburn, whose continued confidence has given me the strength and opportunities to chase all of my dreams. And last, but certainly not least, you the reader – whether you have followed my work online, watched a documentary I directed or simply picked up this book by accident, I wouldn't have made it this far without you.

FOREWORD

I'd like to think since man uttered his first word he has been telling stories for entertainment, to serve as warnings and to simply pass the time. This collection of tales from my home county of Tyne and Wear hopefully reflects a diverse catalogue of some of the stories that may otherwise have been lost to time. While I can't vouch for the complete truth of these stories due to their historic timeframe and reliance on archives, as well as the fact they have come from word-of-mouth accounts, what I can say is that it is up to you the reader what you would like to believe.

CONTENTS

THE AMERICAS

Spreading all over the world, British citizens have left their native country for reasons innumerable. Some have sought more freedom, economic prosperity, and others adventure, with many making the arduous journey to the continents of both North and South America in hopes of changing their fortune. Below are accounts connected to the North East, with some people arriving and others departing, but all are tied to our county of Tyne and Wear.

JOHN TRUMBLE

Whether they were fleeing persecution, or hoping to carve out a piece of land for themselves, the opportunities that the colonisation of America provided drew in people from all over England. One interesting local man who travelled overseas at this time was John Trumble of Newcastle upon Tyne.

Born in 1612, he boarded a ship destined for America and settled in Rowley, Massachusetts. Here he worked as a town clerk and teacher, becoming a respected member of his community. He died in 1687, having been one of the earliest settlers in this part of the world. By choosing to brave the journey and face the unknown, John had started a legacy that rippled on through generations.

Over a number of years, descendants of the Trumble family went on to do great things. John's grandson, Jonathan Trumbull Sr, was the only man to be both governor of an English colony and of an American state. When the Revolutionary War began he was the only governor to take up the patriot cause against the English. In commemoration of the actions he took in his life, a number of places in the USA are named after him.

John Trumbull, son of Jonathan Trumbull Sr, is often referred to as the painter of the revolution. Painting historic scenes from the war, his talents soon made him popular, eventually leading to him painting George Washington. His painting of the Declaration of Independence and other works hang in the United States Capitol rotunda to this day.

While there are still a number of interesting people descendant from the original John Trumbull that I have left out, these are the most famous examples. The impact one Newcastle man had on history by braving the journey and settling into a new life is undoubtable. It does make you wonder though, what John Trumbull would have thought of his grandson's pursuit of an America free from British rule.

SLAVERY AND FREEDOM

Mary Ann Macham was born in Virginia in the United States in 1802 to an enslaved mother and a father who was a slave owner. On a cold Christmas Day in 1831 she arrived in North Shields on board a ship named the *Atlas*, having escaped her cruel life on the plantation back in America.

Though not much is known about her life prior to her arrival, it is possible she may have bought passage across the Atlantic or been helped by a secret organisation known as the Underground Rail Road, who used a number of contacts and safe houses to help more than 10,000 enslaved people flee the southern states to head north.

The *Atlas* initially docked in Grimsby before the ship's captain brought her to the North East, perhaps knowing of sympathetic families that might take her in. The Spence family, who were Quakers, employed her as a domestic servant in the various homes of family members. In 1841, Mary married a local man named James Blyth who worked as a rope maker and later a banker's porter, possibly working for the Spence family bank. The couple lived in various houses on Howard Street in North Shields until James's death in 1877.

After the death of her husband, Mary continued to live in North Shields, staying with relatives of her husband in South Benwell. In 1893, at the age of 91, Mary died and was buried in Preston Village Cemetery, having enjoyed sixty years of freedom.

FREDERICK DOUGLASS

Frederick Douglass, born Frederick Augustus Washington Bailey, was born in 1818 in Cordova, Maryland. After living as a slave for twenty years, Douglass escaped and began campaigning for black emancipation, racial justice and a number of other progressive ideas considered radical at the time. He also started the *North Star* newspaper whilst battling to end segregation in schools.

In August 1846 he arrived in Tyne and Wear as part of a tour where he would give talks. During this visit he spoke at three different locations, one in North Shields, the other two in Newcastle. At this time Newcastle and the North East had a strong abolitionist community, which immediately caught Douglass' attention. He later returned in December of the same year for another two speaking engagements and whilst here stayed with a Quaker family known by the surname Richardson.

In part the Richardson family consisted of Henry, his wife Anna and his sister Ellen. They were well known as abolitionists and activists who at this time took a particular interest in Douglass' case. As he had escaped his former master, payment was required, making him technically an unfree man, something that bothered the Richardson family. Following months of fundraising this small group of Quakers, miles away from Douglass' birthplace, raised enough funds to purchase his freedom and his bill of emancipation was produced.

Though their act was not without its critics, as some believed the purchase legitimised slavery, Douglass was grateful to be able to continue his work back in the United States without fear of being arrested. Douglass spoke in the North East a number of times, always receiving a warm welcome. However, he was not the only former slave to give speeches in the abolitionist circuit in the North. Speaking on his time in Newcastle, Douglas is quoted as saying, 'Newcastle had a heart that could feel for three millions of oppressed slaves in the United States.'

WILLIAM MACDONALD

William Macdonald was born in the West Indies into a life of enslavement sometime during the late 1700s. While little is known about his early years it was a chance encounter at a dock sometime during the early nineteenth century that brought him here. Hearing the sailors there talk of how England was a land of freedom, William set about making his escape.

Concealing himself aboard a ship bound for London, he hid below deck for three days without food. When he made his presence known, to the astonishment of the sailors on board, they gave him food and showed him kindness. An article in the *Nottinghamshire Guardian* on 8 May 1851 tells of his reaction upon landing on English soil, 'As soon as the vessel arrived at London, his love of liberty was so intense that he instantly leaped on shore, though imperfectly clothed, without either money or friends, and with an imperfect knowledge of the English language.'

He eventually made his way up north, deciding to stay in Sunderland, where he reportedly worked at a number of local collieries as a coal hewer. His life was cut short by an accident at Monkwearmouth Colliery in 1851 when rope attached to the tubs broke and he was crushed between another tub, effectively being strangled. William was the only fatality of this accident and the result of the inquest concluded that cold weather had affected the otherwise reliable machinery.

It seems that in Sunderland William MacDonald not only found freedom but acceptance. While slavery had been abolished in Britain some years earlier, it was not until 1833 that it would be abolished elsewhere in the British Empire. The original *Sunderland Herald* article that reported his death describes him as being an industrious man, a member of the Church of England and much respected by his neighbours.

FORGOTTEN ACT OF KINDNESS

The Quaker family known as the Richardsons are well remembered in the county for the generosity they have shown to those most in need. In particular, as mentioned earlier, they helped emancipate fugitive slaves Frederick Douglas and William Wells Brown by purchasing their freedom and allowing them to continue lecturing on the abolitionist circuit. One story that seems to be largely forgotten is the act of kindness they showed to a travelling tribe of Native Americans.

The Ioway Indians were a travelling troupe of Native Americans who toured Europe in the 1800s. Often performing demonstrations of scalping and exhibiting different rituals from their culture, the public frequently regarded them as savages. One place they seem to have found comfort is in the North East with the Richardson family.

The tribe toured Tyne and Wear, visiting a coal pit and seeing local sights. One of their first enquiries upon arriving in Newcastle was if it had a jail; while they had seen prisons before, the concept seemed foreign to them. Their time in the North East is surprisingly well chronicled by George Catlin, who travelled with and recorded them. When the time came for the group to leave they headed towards Scotland, leaving behind the new friends they had made.

Sadly, while travelling in Scotland the child of tribe member Little Wolfe passed away. Born on the Missouri River during the first leg of their journey and named after the boat that brought them to Europe, baby Corsair was not yet a year old. Rather than bury their child as soon as possible, the tribe returned to Newcastle to be among friends.

Anna Richardson, who was instrumental in bringing the group to Newcastle, organised the burial in February 1845 at Westgate Hill Cemetery, where the gravestone is still visible today.

Continuing with their tour, the tribe eventually arrived in Paris, where Corsair's mother also tragically passed away. Thought to have been caused by the grief of the loss of her child, the Ioway Indians returned to America not long after. Thankfully not all of their tour was as tragic, and upon their return they wrote letters describing how they enjoyed the time they spent in the North East and would remember the friends they had made.

AMERICA CIVIL WAR VETERANS

Born in Church Way, North Shields, Robert Rennoldson was a young apprentice on a British shipping vessel when the war between the North and South began. When the ship docked in an American port, Rennoldson, eager for adventure, reportedly left the vessel determined to take part in the fighting.

It is said he came into contact with some farmers who were more interested in tending to their land than engaging in the warfare and who were also offering a bounty to men who would fight in their place. Rennoldson accepted this bounty and fought for five years before returning to the farmer and eventually making his way back to North Shields. Upon his return he secured work as a shipyard labourer, living in his home town into his 70s until he passed away in 1917.

Born in Ireland in 1836, John Pendergast moved to North Shields at a young age, possibly as a result of the famine. Far from being alone, it is estimated 8 per cent of Newcastle's population in 1851 were Irish born. Sometime during the 1850s John travelled to the United States, and in 1862 joined the Northern Army as a private in Captain Lewis Beckworth's company of the 15th Battalion, Connecticut Fusiliers, many of whom were also Irish. John is reported to have seen some hard fighting in places like Port Hudson, along the Red River and in Sheridan's Shenandoah Valley campaign before the war would end.

After three years' active service he was discharged at Savannah in August 1865. He then returned home to North Shields and settled down, residing in Liddell Terrace when he died on 5 May 1901.

Both men are buried in Preston Cemetery, although it was sometime after his death that Robert Rennoldson was recognised as a veteran of the Civil War. Growing interest in commemorating the actions of veterans who had fought in the wars that America was involved in saw an annual ceremony commemorating these and other veterans from the area.

AN AMERICAN CIVIL WAR HERO

George H. Bell was born in Sunderland on 12 March 1839. His family moved to Newcastle shortly after, where George would begin his maritime career aged 14. Over the next seven years George would sail the Atlantic Ocean, Baltic Sea, Black Sea, Caribbean Sea, Indian Ocean and Mediterranean Sea.

During the beginning of the American Civil War in 1861, George was docked at New York City, where he would enlist in the United States Navy. He joined the USS *Santee* and quickly rose through the ranks due to his vast experience at sea.

At Galveston Bay, Texas, on 7 November 1861, the USS *Santee* was tasked with destroying the Confederate Ship *Royal Yacht*. The ship was caught by surprise in the early hours of the morning but the battle was still fierce and is said to have included hand-to-hand combat. The *Santee* suffered one fatality in the skirmish, with the *Royal Yacht* eventually catching fire. Thomas Chubb, the captain of the *Royal Yacht,* was arrested with much of his crew and sent to New York. There he would be sentenced to hang, only to escape the gallows in a prisoner exchange.

In 1863, George was awarded the Medal of Honour in recognition of his service in the United States Military and the conflict with the *Royal Yacht* in particular. He finished out his service and returned to the North East, where he spent much of his life until he died in 1917 and was buried in Newcastle.

KIDNAPPED TO FIGHT IN THE CIVIL WAR

Beginning in 1861, the American Civil War between the North and South over controversial slavery laws saw many men from both sides drafted in to fight. One story that has gone seemingly unnoticed, however, is that British men, often sailors, were press-ganged into fighting for the unionists. Reports in 1864 surfaced detailing the stories of men who had either been brought to America against their will, under false pretences or who had been kidnapped while docked in harbour.

Twenty-six-year-old James Conway was an Irishman who had married and settled in Sunderland. James was one of those unfortunate enough to be press-ganged when, in May of 1863, he was on board the *Coral Queen* docked in New York Harbour. After a few days there he gained permission to go ashore and visited a public house in Water Street, where he had a small amount to drink. The next thing he knew he woke up in a village in the state of Ohio wearing military uniform and destined to join the 6th Hampshire Regiment under General Grant. His drink had been drugged. Despite James protesting that he had been made a soldier against his will, he was informed that a bounty had been paid for him and that he would be compelled to stay and fight. Arriving outside an encampment in Nashville, he stayed there for roughly six weeks before being made a sentry and stealthily escaping during the night.

Travelling by steamboat as a stowaway, he made his way to Indiana, getting out before the boat reached its destination of Pennsylvania so as not to be caught as a deserter. He continued on foot, surviving on little food and getting the occasional few days' work as a labourer until a democrat took pity on him, taking him in for a few days, feeding him and also changing his clothes. In Pittsburgh he again worked as a labourer for a few weeks, saving up enough money to get a train back to New York, where he managed to gain passage on board a ship bound for Liverpool. Upon his arrival he immediately had to go to hospital to recover from the hardships he had endured, and after leaving managed to make his way home to Sunderland on another boat. James Conway was gone for over a year with no way of contacting his family, leaving them in a terrible state of suspense as to his fate. In a letter in which he described his ordeal he stated that following his forced adventure he changed career and became involved in the coal trade.

Another letter, from a Sunderland man named William Downs, described how he was also forcibly enlisted while also docked in New York. William told how he had been enlisted in the navy for three years and that he would soon be sent to join a blockade. Though William did not seem to mind too much, stating that it was a good opportunity to make money, he told how he hoped the war would soon come to an end and that he would be discharged before his three years' service. In the letter he also mentioned a friend named William Johnson who had been enlisted in the army but gave no more information.

This final story of Civil War kidnapping is that of an apprentice in the barque *Resolution* of Sunderland, belonging to Messrs Nicholson & Son. While his name was not mentioned a letter that reached a man named Captain Brunton, he told in it how during his time docked at New York he was enticed to desert his vessel and go to a boarding house under the promise of a job paying more money. Only a few days later he too was drugged and woke up to find himself enrolled in the Federal Army. This man, whose name was not mentioned, was wounded at Spotsylvania Court House on 12 May 1864, but by July his wounds were said to have healed. Terrified of being sent to the front again, he wrote to Captain Brunton, begging for enough money to make his way to New York and then safety. Captain Brunton obliged this request and sent the money but had to leave soon after and the report stated the fate of this man was unknown.

It was not only Sunderland men who were unfortunate enough to be forcibly enlisted to fight in the American Civil War, as reports of these strange practices seem nationwide. While these events seem to have been almost entirely forgotten, it is my opinion that it would certainly make an exciting movie. James Conway was likely one of few men to escape his forced adventure and there will have been many who were not so lucky.

ULYSSES S. GRANT

Ulysses S. Grant arrived in Newcastle on 20 September 1877. Thousands of spectators came to watch his arrival and during his time in the North East many of his appearances drew huge crowds. Grant's achievements during the end of the American Civil War saw him re-elected as president and made him famous across the world.

On his second day he toured Tynemouth, meeting local South Shields MP James Cochran Stevenson and taking in a display by the local Lifeboat Brigade. On the evening in question he attended the performance of a specially written play entitled *North and South! An Episode of Vicksburg*, about the forbidden love between a Union officer and the daughter of a Confederate general. Before leaving Newcastle a parade was thrown in his honour, during which he made a speech to an audience of more than 80,000 people.

Ulysses S. Grant arrived in Monkwearmouth train station on his third day into his visit in the North East. He had written to the mayor prior to his visit requesting that a holiday be granted to shopkeepers on the day of his arrival, which was permitted. During his visit to Sunderland the foundation stone for the Museum and Winter Gardens was laid in his presence commemorating the event, during which he toured many parts of the local industry.

The eighteenth President of the United States left for Sheffield a few days later to continue his tour of the world. Ulysses S. Grant was said to have enjoyed his time in the North East and made his appreciation known while speaking to the press: 'I have had no better reception in any place, nor do I think it possible to have a better. All I have seen since I have been on the Tyne has been to me most gratifying as an individual.'

Did you know that in 1977, President of the United States of America Jimmy Carter paid a visit to Newcastle? In an effort to strengthen ties between the USA and England, there was an exchange of travellers and Carter was keen to see Newcastle for himself.

MUHAMMAD ALI

In that same year of 1977, boxing legend Muhammad Ali flew into Newcastle Airport. Spending four days in the area accompanied by his then wife Veronica, the couple visited a mosque in South Shields to have their marriage blessed. Invited by former South Shields boxer Johnny Walker, who had flown to America to ask Ali in person if he would visit, 'the Greatest' obliged and showed great kindness in helping a cause to raise money for a local boxing club. Visiting at the peak of his career, locals turned out in their thousands with slack jaws, not quite believing that they could get so close to such a legend. He would become heavyweight boxing champion of the world three times, no doubt making his visit even more unforgettable to those who were lucky enough to experience it.

BUFFALO BILL IN THE NORTH EAST

William Frederick Cody, also known as Buffalo Bill, was born in 1846 in what is now the state of Iowa in the United States. Bill started working at the age of 11, and became a rider for the Pony Express not long after before serving in the American Civil War. Bill is believed to have received his nickname from his time spent contracted to providing the Kansas City Railroad with buffalo meat, during which he is estimated to have killed 4,282 buffalo in eighteen months.

In December 1872 he made his stage debut in a Wild West show, before going on to form his own group and touring the states. Having visited the UK previously on a tour, he returned in 1904 and performed in a number of places he had not visited previously. Four of those locations were Newcastle, North Shields, South Shields and Sunderland.

During his stay in Newcastle on this tour Buffalo Bill performed twelve times, setting up camp on the town moor, and it was reported to have attracted more than 14,000 people, with many coming from afar to see it. His show in North Shields was set up on a field near

Linskill Terrace and some spectators even watched from the tower of the Wesleyan Memorial Church in the hope of a better view. At Buffalo Bill's invitation the Mayor of Cardiff attended this performance, as the two had been previously acquainted, occupying a special box. During an interval of this performance he was interviewed about his abstinence from alcohol. He said:

> I am an abstainer, and have been for some years past. I was led to abandon alcoholic liquors because I found it best for health, purse, reputation, and, more especially, as an example to those under me. I insist upon sobriety very strictly, because in work like ours it is absolutely necessary. Horsemanship and skill with the rifle demand it.

The show in South Shields equally captivated its audience as they sat watching the Rough Riders of the World perform fantastic feats. His show featured people from all over the globe such as South Americans, Japanese and Native American warriors. Johnny Baker, a member of his troupe, was particularly acknowledged during this report for his ability to shoot multiple glass balls out of the air at once while on horseback. The report details the most memorable act of his South Shields performance being the cowboy cyclist named Carter. Carter plunged down a specially built platform on his bike and jumped a gap of 55ft, causing an uproar in the audience.

In Sunderland reports detail how Bill's three trains pulled into Monkwearmouth Station, almost immediately drawing crowds of thousands as they made their journey to Lane Ends Farm. Bill was said to be a very friendly man and welcomed visitors. He enquired if there were any veterans of the Indian Wars in America, to which he was surprised to find out a man named Chas Berry, a resident of Harrogate Street, was involved in the Mexican–American War (1846–48) and invited him to attend the show.

Entertainment has changed a great deal since the days of Buffalo Bill and his Wild West show, but I believe that there are few today who would not have found this an amazing show to attend.

STAN LEE

While many are familiar with the creator of Marvel characters popularised in comic and cinematic form, few are aware of his distant relationship with Newcastle. Joan Boocock Lee was born in Gosforth, Newcastle, in 1922. She moved to the USA after the Second World War, having married an American serviceman whom she had only known for twenty-four hours prior to their wedding. Originally a well-known hat model in the UK, she separated from her husband shortly after their relocation to America. Rumour has it that Stan Lee's cousin had set him up on a blind date with a different model from the same place where Joan worked; however, after Joan opened the door to him he fell head over heels for her. Stan Lee proposed after two weeks of dating and she went to Reno, Nevada, to nullify her previous marriage. Staying together to the end, Joan is credited with the early inspiration for The Fantastic Four. She passed away in 2017 aged 95 and Stan Lee also sadly died only a year later. Their legacy will no doubt continue to live on for years to come.

THE REVOLT OF THE LASH

The Revolt of the Lash is a mutiny that took place among the Brazilian Navy in late November 1910. This broke out as a direct result of the use of whips by white naval officers when punishing Afro-Brazilian and dual-heritage sailors. Shortly before this, two ships were constructed for the Brazilian Navy by Armstrong Whitworth at Elswick. They were the *Minas Gerais*, thought to be the most powerful dreadnought battleship in the world at the time, and the *Bahia*, which was considered the fastest cruiser.

During the construction of these ships as many as 1,000 sailors of mostly African descent found themselves in Newcastle training to serve as crew. Brazil became the last country in the Western Hemisphere to abolish slavery in 1888, and as such many of the sailors would have been former slaves or had parents who were slaves, meaning they endured hard lives and harsh treatment in the navy. Some of the men stationed in Newcastle were there for as much as seven months and many groups were housed together in boarding houses or rented smaller flats together. Here in Newcastle these men experienced a level of economic opportunity and freedom that was generally out of reach to them in Rio de Janeiro. Their extra wages, as well as the fact that they were able to interact with and observe the working classes of Newcastle, will have no doubt reinforced their grievances and contributed to their determination for a revolt.

Known for their tradition of popular radicalism throughout the nineteenth century, the visiting sailors experienced two strikes by Newcastle workers during the building of the Brazilian ships. This example of workers' unity and organised resistance would have also not gone unnoticed by these men. At this time Newcastle also had a reputation for anti-racism and as the city depended a great deal economically on the business of building ships like this, foreigners were often warmly welcomed in the city for the money they brought. The British consul in Brazil, Ernest Hambloch, later described an interaction with three young women from Newcastle who came to his office requesting to be returned home, with their husbands' consent, as they were not being taken care of in Brazil.

When the ships arrived in Brazil in 1910, a carefully planned mutiny was executed and the *Minas Gerais'* mighty weapons were aimed at Rio with the threat of unleashing chaos. The crews' control of these two ships and others saw the remaining Brazilian Navy's firepower dwarfed and they sent their demands to the president. Led by João Cândido Felisberto, who it is believed was strongly influenced by his experiences on Tyneside, they requested an end to what they described as slavery within the navy and amnesty for those involved. Though the revolt was not entirely peaceful and some officers and other men were killed in the initial clash, the demands of those involved were met. Despite amnesty being granted, many of those involved were later arrested or sent to work camps, including the leader João, who was tortured.

The radicalism, unity and freedom the sailors experienced in Newcastle and surrounding areas undoubtedly had an impact on them and is just one of many examples of how the North East and its people have influenced and changed the world.

CREATIVES

Creativity comes in many forms and it can earn its keeper a place of high regard throughout time. Whether born here in the North East or a legendary figure passing through, you can find evidence of these sparks spotted throughout our well-documented history in Tyne and Wear. While not every tale can be told in this book, some of these fascinating cases are documented for you to view in the following pages.

DICKENS IN SUNDERLAND

In August 1852, Charles Dickens made an appearance at Sunderland's New Lyceum Theatre in Lambton Street as part of a comedy show raising funds for writers.

The performance drew a crowd of more than 1,200 and it was a concern that too many people would attend. The theatre had only just finished construction work and the large audience caused Dickens to fear for his life. A day after attending the show, the author wrote to his friend John Foster about his experience in Sunderland:

> When we got here at noon it appeared that the hall was a perfectly new one and had only had the slates put upon the roof by torchlight over-night.

Further, proprietors of some opposition rooms had declared the building unsafe, and there was a panic in the town about it; people having had their money back.

I didn't know what to do. The horrible responsibility of risking an accident of that awful nature seemed to rest only upon me ...

The only comfort I had was in stumbling at length on the builder, and found him a plain practical North Countryman, with a foot rule in his pocket.

I took him aside and asked him should we, or could we, prop up any weak part of the place. He told me that there wasn't a stronger building in the world.

Although Dickens may have been concerned with the safety at the time, judging by his letter he was pleased with the response. 'They (the audience) began with a round of applause when Coote's white waistcoat appeared in the orchestra, and wound up the farce with deafening cheers,' he wrote.

'I never saw such good fellows.'

Did you know that William Terrence Deary, more commonly known as Terry Deary, the author of the popular book series *Horrible Histories*, was born in Sunderland?

LUCOZADE

In 1927, Newcastle pharmacist William Owen created the drink Glucozade in his Barras Bridge shop as an energy source for the sick. Owen experimented for many years to try and provide a source of energy for those sick with common illnesses like the cold and influenza.

Another man often credited with the invention is Professor Frederick Charles Pybus, who was renowned in the medical field. Remembered for his contributions to cancer research, pediatrics and surgical education, Pybus would encourage his patients to drink a glucose-based formula before and after surgery to help break down the anaesthetic and provide energy. William Owen provided the ingredients for the prescription and once it began gaining in popularity decided to perfect the recipe himself.

Glucozade became a success and was used by hospitals throughout Britain. In 1929 the drink was renamed Lucozade and it became a symbol of recovery. In the 1980s it was rebranded as a sports energy drink rather than being associated with illness, and this further increased its success.

JIMI HENDRIX

On 1 February 1967, The Jimi Hendrix Experience played at the New Cellar Club in Thomson Street, South Shields. The cost of entry to the gig was 6s, with local band The Bond supporting. At the time Hendrix was not a huge star but his recently released song 'Hey Joe' was quickly climbing the charts. This was one of the first shows of the tour.

HOUDINI

In February 1904, famous magician and escapologist Harry Houdini arrived in South Shields to perform at the Empire Theatre. During his stay he decided to prove his skills, as he had done in many other places in the country, by breaking out of the local police cell.

On 9 February, he travelled to South Shields Central to meet his audience, which included select members of the Watch Committee and a few of their close friends. He was marched to the cell by Superintendent Cowe and reportedly stripped naked before being handcuffed in front of the audience of policemen using three different types of handcuffs. The different restraints used to see he would not escape were one regulation set of handcuffs, an American patent bracelet style and a figure of eight style. He was then taken to a different cell – his

clothes were left in the original – and sealed in with a triple lock before the cells were inspected at Houdini's request. The inside of the cell door was sheeted with a quarter-inch iron plate that was bolted down and had no access to the lock on the inside.

Before the spectators were led away Houdini remarked, 'I don't say I'll do it but I'll try.' With that the audience was sealed outside an iron gate waiting for the situation to develop. Surely enough, it was said not to have been long before the sound of handcuffs falling could be heard along with the cells being unlocked. Houdini emerged only a few moments later fully dressed, having unlocked both cells and declared himself a free man. Despite his quick escape after this stunt he remarked that the cells in South Shields were exceptionally good and strong. This was roughly the fifty-second escape he had made from cells in this country, but it is one I'm sure the police in South Shields did not forget.

Houdini also made several trips to Newcastle from 1909 to 1920.

In April 1913, he performed a stunt where he dived from a buttress off the Swing Bridge into the river, 15ft below, with his hands manacled behind his back and his arms chained to his side.

Popular legend has it that while at Newcastle Castle, Houdini was challenged to escape the so-called Condemned Cell (which to this day remains closed to the public). However, uncharacteristically he turned it down.

THE NINTH WONDER OF THE WORLD

Hadji Ali is a world-renowned performance artist known for his seemingly original act of controlled regurgitation. Little is known about Ali's early years but he is believed to have been born sometime between 1887 and 1892, and is thought to have been of Egyptian descent, though it is possible he may have been born in another Middle Eastern country.

Although he was not very famous in his time, Ali performed in many countries in different parts of the world and also performed in front of

Russian Tsar Nicholas II. His ability to control his stomach and throat muscles allowed him to swallow many objects and regurgitate them at will. The most infamous part of his act was the finale, where he would swallow a deadly amount of water followed by a bottle of kerosene, which would sit on top of the water in his stomach. He would then regurgitate the kerosene in a flamethrower-like effect, usually igniting a model building, before bringing the water up to put out the fire. This particular trick was recorded in the Laurel and Hardy film *Politiquerias*, and because of this illusionist David Blaine described him as his hero, going to extreme lengths to teach himself the skill.

In September 1937, Ali performed in Sunderland at the Empire Theatre as part of his tour of England, during which he was billed as the ninth wonder of the world on many advertisements. Although I could not find a great deal of information on his performances in the North East, he reportedly also played in Newcastle. A news article describing how firemen watching a demonstration in Birmingham forced him to cut down on the amount of kerosene used, unlike his performance in Newcastle, confirms this.

Ali's performance in Sunderland in September 1937 would unfortunately be one of his last. Two months later, while in Wolverhampton, Ali died from heart failure during a bout of bronchitis most likely brought on from his act. It would have no doubt been an interesting performance for those people of the North East who were lucky enough to see it, and his ability continues to amaze people, even someone such as David Blaine.

Did you know that a President of the United States was assassinated while watching a play written by someone from Sunderland?

Tom Taylor was born in Bishopwearmouth in Sunderland on 19 October 1817. He was a famous playwright during his life and wrote *Our American Cousin*, which Abraham Lincoln was watching at the time of his assassination.

SAVE THE PRESIDENT

On a related note, another local man was present at the time of Abraham Lincoln's assassination and in fact tried to save him. Born in 1834, William Henry Hall was the son of Reverend John Netherton O'Brien Hall, who was an incumbent of St Bede's Church in Jarrow. Growing up, William will have no doubt heard tales of his grandfather John Stephens Hall, who was vice admiral of the Blue Division during the times of Horatio Nelson. It might have been these stories that encouraged him to live an adventurous life and one that would lead him to cross paths with one of the United States' most famous presidents.

While there is little information on William's early years, it is reported that at the young age of 16 he took the brave step of travelling overseas to America. There he settled into a job as a grocer in Memphis, Tennessee. However, it would not be long before the Civil War broke out. In an interview in the *Jarrow Express* in 1916 he describes the events:

> At the time the war between the North and the South broke out I had built quite a comfortable business in Memphis, Tennessee. It was left to the inhabitants of each town to vote whether they would secede from the Union or not. Voting was taken by all those in favour putting lights in their windows at night. I put none in mine, and was asked the reason. I said I was an Englishman and had no desire to enter into a quarrel, and, moreover, if I had, I didn't want to secede. My shop and stock, worth between £2,000 and £3,000, was all taken from me and I left town. I went straight to Chicago, where I enlisted with the Northern Army of Potomac.

After enlisting William was placed in McLellan's Dragoons, which was a cavalry unit. An accident that occurred while he was getting off his horse saw him sent to Chestnut Hill Hospital in Philadelphia to recover. While he was still in uniform he visited Ford's Theatre in Washington on the same night Abraham Lincoln was there. He was sat almost directly under the president in his uniform when he heard the fatal shot fired by assassin John Wilkes Booth.

William, along with three other men, immediately ran to the injured president's aid. Lincoln was lifted on to a shutter and transported to a nearby lodging house for medical attention by William and the others. He died the following day. The events William bore witness to made a clear impact on him, as some years later he attended a showing of the play *The Birth of a Nation* at the Tyne Theatre and remarked at being astounded at the reproduction of events.

William Henry Hall was living in Seafield Terrace in South Shields when he died aged 89. He is buried in Harton Cemetery in South Shields beneath a military gravestone that details his involvement in the United States Civil War.

BREAK A LEG

For many years, the theatre was the cultural centre of towns and cities across the North East, bringing entertainment from parts of the world that were normally out of reach to its working-class residents and providing relief from the stresses of everyday life. The theatre, however, was not always a safe place it seems, and a number of stories in local papers detail the accidents that happened there.

Some may have heard of the more famous incidents such as the death of Robert Crowther, whose skull was crushed after a cannon ball, normally rolled along the rafters to create the sound of lightning, fell and landed on his head at the Tyne Theatre in 1887. Another fairly well-known incident was a fire at the Old Theatre Royal in Newcastle in 1823 that caused a panic and stampede for the exit and resulted in a number of people being crushed to death. Unfortunately, these accidents were far from the only ones to occur in our local theatres.

During a performance of the pantomime *Robin Hood* at the Lyceum Theatre in Sunderland in 1866 an accident led to the death of a young actress. After a cable connecting the gas supply was accidentally unhooked, an employee lit a flame for light, assuming it had been fixed, causing a roar of flames to ignite the performer. Her father, a man named Mr Ricardo, who was also a clown in the show, frantically attempted to put her out with other employees but she died shortly after. At the Palace Theatre in Sunderland, a member of a Japanese gymnastics troupe named Teru Fugi was seriously hurt while performing acrobatic feats atop a tall pole in 1914. Despite having his fall broken by a fellow performer's hand, the acrobat hit his head on the stage and was taken to hospital.

In 1920, at the New Pavilion Theatre on Westgate Road in Newcastle, a man's enthusiasm for the show he was watching would see him suffer a nasty injury. At the conclusion of the performance, the National Anthem was played and the spectator leaned over the partition separating the audience from the orchestra to speak to some of the players. As he was doing so he failed to notice the curtain drop and had his head squashed between the curtain and the top rail of the partition. He remained trapped there until stage hands managed to rescue him, reportedly sustaining serious injuries to the head and neck.

THE IWAKURA MISSION

The Iwakura Mission was a Japanese diplomatic voyage across Europe and the United States of America between 1871 and 1873, with the purpose of renegotiating trade deals and gaining knowledge to help with the modernisation of the home country. The delegation of leading scholars and statesmen, from the Meiji period, arrived in the UK a year into their trip in 1872. Visiting a number of important cities all over the country, the group arrived in Newcastle on 21 October.

While in Newcastle, the party stayed at the Royal Station Hotel, venturing out to tour local industries. The men visited Gosforth mines, Elswick Ordnance Works and the Newcastle and Gateshead Chamber of Commerce. They also took part in a boat ride down the Tyne, travelling as far as Hebburn and Jarrow. The part of the visit the group benefited most from is arguably their visit to Elswick, where they had the opportunity to visit Sir William Armstrong's armament factory.

The group were escorted from their hotel by Sir Armstrong to his plant, where they saw the different departments at first hand. Following the tour, the group were also given a demonstration of a Gatling gun constructed there. This visit forged a lasting relationship between Japan and Armstrong, which began supplying his trademarked Armstrong Gun almost immediately after their return. Their relationship continued for several years and Armstrong supplied much of the country's military firepower, including warships used in the Russo-Japanese War.

Although this was not the first delegation from Japan to arrive in Newcastle it is recognised as being very important in the history of that country's modernisation. After a period of isolation from the West it is interesting to think what these visitors made of the North East and its people.

JOSEPH CONRAD

Born in 1857, Joseph Conrad was a Polish novelist who is perhaps most famous for *Heart of Darkness*. Writing near the peak of the British Empire, Conrad's novels often featured a nautical setting and were written in English, despite him not learning to speak it until he was in his 20s.

Spending a great deal of time at sea, Conrad first arrived in England at Lowestoft, where he signed on for a number of voyages transporting coal to and from Newcastle in 1878. It is believed that during these trips he began learning English, likely mixing with some people from the North East. Only a few years later, in 1881, he set sail for Newcastle on board the *Palestine* as second mate to transport coal to Bangkok. Gales prevented the ship from reaching the Tyne for sixteen days and it was later rammed by a steam vessel before berthing. When the *Palestine* eventually set sail it sprung a leak in the English Channel and became stuck in Falmouth, Cornwall. In regard to this chain of unfortunate events, Conrad had this to say of his captain: 'Poor old Captain Beard looked like a ghost of a Geordie skipper.'

The story of the *Palestine* is thought to be the basis for his novel *Youth*, although the ship's name is changed to *Judea*. Rising through the ranks, his experience at sea not only saw him recognised through promotions but also inspired his writing.

One of his last voyages at sea before beginning his literary career was as chief officer on board the *Torrens*, built by James Laing of Sunderland. Considered by some to be the finest ship ever launched from a Sunderland yard, her speed was said to be unmatched and she covered 16,000 miles in a record-breaking run to Adelaide. He had this to say of the ship:

A ship of brilliant qualities – the way the ship had of letting big seas slip under her did one's heart good to watch. It resembled so much an exhibition of intelligent grace and unerring skill that it could fascinate even the least seamanlike of our passengers.

Conrad's books inspired numerous authors and filmmakers decades after his death. Arguably the most famous example of this is the film *Apocalypse Now*, which reimagines his novel *Heart of Darkness* in the setting of the Vietnam War.

INVENTING THE LIFEBOAT

The lifeboat is an invention undoubtedly responsible for saving countless lives but it has not always existed to help those in troubled waters. The idea of the lifeboat as we know it was born in South Shields, although its inventor is widely contested. Wrecks were common on the North East coast and were the inspiration for a competition to find a boat design that could save lives in 1790.

Henry Greathead is largely credited with being the inventor, his lifeboat having come first in the competition. It was not until 1802 that his design was deemed fit for national use and Henry was awarded £1,200 by Parliament for his invention by petitioning it with the claim he had invented the boat in 1790.

William Wouldhave was born in North Shields in 1751 and then moved to South Shields, where he would meet and marry his wife, Hannah Crow. William did not succeed with the practical application of his lifeboat design until 1789 and also entered the competition, only to come second. William contested that Henry was the true inventor of the lifeboat, claiming that he had designed it earlier, with the only difference in design being the curved keel of the boat. It was not until Henry's petition of Parliament that he was widely recognised as the inventor.

It is believed Wouldhave's claims to the invention were hampered by his use of bad language and the poverty in which he lived. Many people backed his claims, citing his letters and paperwork as evidence, though it continued to be reported in the media that Henry Greathead was the inventor. William died in 1821 and was buried in St Hilda's Church graveyard in South Shields, where a memorial stands today. Henry Greathead never took out a patent for his invention and shared his work for the good of the public.

The question of who was the true inventor of the lifeboat is hard to answer but what is known is that countless sailors owe their lives to both of these men.

DAREDEVIL SCHREYER

Max Schreyer was an American daredevil cyclist and athlete born sometime in the nineteenth century. Between 1885 and 1919 he travelled the world performing his amazing feats, eventually arriving in the UK. In 1906 he came to Newcastle to perform his most famous stunt, which involved riding a bicycle down a ramp that was more than 100ft tall then propelling himself off and landing in a tank filled with water.

Schreyer was booked by the proprietor Richard Thornton for a season at the Olympia Theatre in Newcastle beginning on 30 April. There was a problem, however, as the building was too small to house his amazing trick, so to make it possible a portion of the roof was removed. This meant that when he began his performance he started outside in front of crowds of pedestrians all eager to catch a glimpse of the famous daredevil, with the number of spectators being reported to be as many as 15,000. Not only were the streets packed but the theatre itself was also stated to be crowded to the doors. Once he climbed to the lofty height he rode down at a speed of roughly 80mph before flying off and landing in the tank successfully. Emerging from his watery safety net to a thunderous round of applause, he would then perform again. Thornton gave a speech afterwards declaring Schreyer's performance the greatest in the world, before saying it was worth double the money he paid.

The daredevil continued touring the world to arenas and theatres packed with thousands of people for a good number of years. In May 1919 his luck unfortunately changed when he suffered a fatal accident. While performing at Van Cortlandt Park in New York in front of 20,000 people, including his wife and infant son, he struck the side of the tank and was injured. He survived a few days in hospital before succumbing to his injuries.

It is hard to imagine a feat like this being performed now and it no doubt stuck with the people of Newcastle who were lucky enough to see it.

MAD MADGE, THE DUCHESS OF NEWCASTLE

Margaret Lucas was born in 1623 into a family of prominent Royalists. When Queen Henrietta Maria, wife of Charles I, was exiled to France following the execution of her husband, Margaret followed and lived for a time in Paris. It was here against the advice of her peers that she married William Cavendish, the 1st Duke of Newcastle, in 1645.

Seen by many at the time as an eccentric for a number of reasons, Margaret cursed, flirted and designed her own clothes. This caught the attention of fellow aristocrats, whose opinions were divided on her. After the restoration of the monarchy in England, Margaret and her husband returned and set about restoring the Cavendish estates.

At a time when there were very few women writers and those that published did so anonymously, Margaret was publishing numerous works under her own name. Her diverse works included poems, essays, plays and fictional stories. Many also credit her with being one of the first early science fiction writers because of her book named *The Blazing World* in which the character, also named Margaret Cavendish, enters a utopian world through the North Pole and meets a variety of talking animals.

The centre of new science, the Royal Society of London, which did not admit women, invited her to visit in 1667 and she watched a number of scientific demonstrations. The next time a woman would be permitted to visit by the society was centuries away and it was not until 1945 that it had its first female member.

While the likes of Samuel Pepys, noted for his diary that detailed the Great Fire of London, did not appreciate her efforts, many were astounded by her. The nickname Mad Madge appears to be something that followed after her lifetime, although she was a renowned eccentric in her time. Cavendish died in 1673 and was buried in Westminster Abbey, followed shortly by her husband two years later. He was said to be proud of her to the end. Margaret Cavendish is remembered as a pioneer and a woman well ahead of her time.

THE GHOSTS OF FAFFNER HALL

While many people are familiar with Jim Henson and his role in creating the legendary television and film puppet characters the Muppets, very few people will know about a largely forgotten chapter in Jim Henson history that took place in Newcastle. *The Ghosts of Faffner Hall* was a Jim Henson Company creation filmed in the now closed Tyne Tees Television Studios during the 1980s.

Jim Henson was born and studied in the USA but when he created the first two pilot episodes of *The Muppet Show* he could not find an audience for them there. Instead, *The Muppet Show* was produced in the UK at Elstree Studios in Hertfordshire, where it ran for five series. Henson's talent was recognised and he began to work on a variety of film and television projects, one of which was *The Ghosts of Faffner Hall*.

This was a television show aimed at getting young people interested in different types of music. Throughout its only series a number of guest stars appeared on the show such as Joni Mitchell, James Taylor and Ladysmith Black Mambazo. All the Muppets used were created by the Jim Henson Creature Shop and many episodes featured characters from *The Muppet Show*. Tyne Tees Television Studios has since moved near to the Metrocentre in Gateshead. Henson's unexpected death in 1991 was a big shock to the film and television community and he is remembered for the joy he brought to children everywhere.

Did you know that actor Liam Neeson is rumoured to have trained as a teacher in the now closed St Mary's College in Fenham, Newcastle?

On this same theme, actor Rowan Atkinson, who is perhaps most famous for his roles in the television shows *Blackadder* and *Mr Bean,* also studied in Newcastle. Graduating in 1975 with a degree in Electrical and Electronic Engineering before being catapulted into fame, he had his humble beginnings in the North East, being born in Consett, County Durham.

MADAME JO GIRARDELLI

Jo Girardelli was a popular circus performer who was born in Italy during the 1780s. She toured through some of Europe before arriving in Britain. She travelled up and down the country, visiting Newcastle in 1818, leaving audiences stunned at her talents.

Her show would start with a trick involving nitric acid. She would take a mouthful and swish it around for some time before spitting it onto an iron bar, which would then melt in front of the gasping crowd. The next trick she would perform would be to boil water in which she would cook an egg as proof of its legitimacy before again swishing the scalding hot water in her mouth and spitting it out. Girardelli would also allegedly put molten lead into her mouth and spit out solidified, coin-sized pieces, often getting a volunteer from the audience to check inside her mouth for signs of damage.

To prove it was not only her mouth that could withstand extreme heat, she would also take a shovel and heat it in a fire until it became red hot. She would then proceed to press it against various parts of her body before finally putting it on her tongue. Sceptics and scientists all tried to debunk the act but no rational explanation was ever found. Madame Girardelli left England soon after her sudden rise to fame. She then seemed to disappear, with there being no record of her life after her departure.

It would be interesting to know what the people of Newcastle thought of Madame Girardelli, the Fireproof Phenomenon.

THE MAN WHO PERFORMED FOR HITLER

Born in 1901 in Melbourne as Leo Norman Maurien Murray Stuart Carrington Walters, developing the stage name Murray the Escapologist later, his career as a conjurer began at the early age of 14. Murray was soon touring the world and became increasingly popular after the death of Houdini in 1926, when he was recognised as coming up with the term 'escapologist'.

Some of Murray's most famous tricks included Shooting Through a Woman, the Pin Cushion Girl, Siberian Handcuff Escape, Girl Without a Middle, and the show would often climax with him escaping from a slotted box while immersed in water.

In 1937, Murray performed at the now long-demolished Blacks Regal Theatre in Sunderland. As part of the build-up to the show he was driven around town suspended upside down in a straitjacket with his feet fastened together before he managed to escape.

His constant touring made him one of the most well-travelled performers of his time. When the Second World War broke out Murray was performing in Berlin at the Wintergarten before Hermann Göering and Adolf Hitler. Murray fled Germany shortly after with a female member of his crew, leaving behind 20 tonnes of equipment. He retired from show business in 1954 due to ill health and moved to Blackpool, where he opened a magic shop and lived until he passed away in 1989.

YEVGENY ZAMYATIN

Born in 1884 in Lebedyan, almost 200 miles from Moscow in Russia, Zamyatin was an author of science fiction and political satire. Son to an Orthodox priest, he enrolled in naval engineering studies between 1902 and 1908, spending some of that time at St Petersburg. Joining the Bolsheviks during this time, he was arrested during the Russian Revolution of 1905 and was exiled, staying illegally in St Petersburg for some months after. He was eventually forced to flee and made his way to Finland to continue his studies but was later granted amnesty and returned to his home country. It was not long before he was arrested again in 1911 and exiled once more, only to be pardoned in 1913, which is when his literary career began to take form.

Having graduated as an engineer for the Imperial Russian Navy, he travelled to Newcastle upon Tyne to supervise the building of Russian ice-breakers. It was here that he witnessed the city being bombed by Zeppelins during the First World War. Visiting South Shields, Sunderland and different parts of Newcastle during this period, his novel *Islanders* satirised the English bourgeoisie he encountered. While some argue that Zamyatin did not enjoy his time here, another published recollection of local author Harold Heslop, from County Durham, suggests otherwise. This quote is an extract from the mentioned publication by Alan Myers:

> On Heslop's remarking that he preferred South Shields to Newcastle, Zamyatin whispered 'South Shields ... Sooth Sheels! I never learned to sing the Tyneside speech!' These are not the words of the scourge of the Newcastle middle classes nor the glum introvert of the letters to his wife. Zamyatin's affection for the ordinary Geordie and his informed interest in the local dialect is obviously genuine.

Zamyatin returned once more to Russia to take part in the continuing revolution but would become increasingly critical of Bolshevik censorship. His most famous work, *We*, envisioned a dystopian police state and this would later become inspiration for George Orwell's *1984*. Orwell also argued that *We* had been inspiration for Aldous Huxley's *Brave New World,* something Huxley denied. Zamyatin's writing eventually became too critical for the state to tolerate and with Stalin's permission he left with his family to live in Paris. It was here that in 1937, aged 53, he died of a heart attack while living in poverty.

OSCAR WILDE

Born in Dublin, Ireland, Oscar Fingal O'Flahertie Wills Wilde is a well-known playwright, poet and author. Perhaps most renowned for his book *The Picture of Dorian Gray* and his play *The Importance of Being Ernest*, Wilde was already well known before they were published.

Visiting Sunderland in 1884, he gave a lecture to a packed audience, which included the mayor, in Victoria Hall. Focusing on aestheticism, a movement in which the beauty of art is seen through its aesthetic value rather than deeper meaning, he discussed home decor and fashion. He is described as having worn a black and white suit with a strawberry-coloured handkerchief thought to be there purely for aesthetic purposes. During the lecture he also praised the necessity of the youth learning craftsmanship, declaring England would never have beautiful furniture until we recognised handicraft. The following week he returned to Victoria Hall and gave another well-attended lecture on his impressions of America, which was described as being most enjoyable, with the language and the style being described as artistic.

In 1885 he visited Newcastle, lecturing at the Tyne Theatre on the subject of dress. His presence was again a sell-out affair, with a number of people attempting to attend being refused entry. During this lecture he praised the Greek style of garments hanging from the shoulder rather than the waist. He also discussed the slavery of fashion, stating that the current mode of dress arose from its mutability. Going into detail about Egyptian and Greek styles, he pointed out how such countries' choice of clothing had been in the same fashion for centuries.

When his play *The Importance of Being Ernest* was at its peak he attempted to prosecute the Marquess of Queensberry, a Scottish noble, with criminal libel. The Marquess was father to Wilde's lover, Lord Alfred Douglass. During the trial evidence of his homosexuality was unearthed and Wilde was forced to stand trial for gross indecency. Sentenced to two years' hard labour, the maximum sentence, he was imprisoned from 1895 to 1897.

Upon his release he left for France, never to return to Britain, where he wrote his last work, *The Ballad of Reading Gaol*. It is thought he never properly recovered from his time in prison and as a result he died only a couple of years later, in 1900, destitute in Paris. Only in 2017 was he posthumously pardoned alongside 50,000 other men who had been convicted of crimes relating to homosexual acts.

BLONDIN IN THE NORTH EAST

Charles Blondin, born Jean François Gravelet, was a French tightrope walker renowned the world over for his amazing feats. Perhaps best known for his achievements in the United States, where he traversed Niagara Falls on a tightrope, he also performed all kinds of other amazing stunts such as cooking himself an omelette while on the rope, tightrope walking blindfolded, carrying his manager on his back and also standing on a chair with one leg balancing on the rope. All these phenomenal feats cemented his reputation as a daredevil who did not know the meaning of fear.

While he is thought by many to be the world's best tightrope walker, there are few who know about his visits to the North East, where he appeared in Newcastle in 1861 and Hendon Vale, Sunderland, the same year.

In August 1862, Blondin returned to the North East and visited the cricket field in North Shields to show off his unique acrobatic talent. While he was prevented from performing on the initially planned day due to the weather, he followed through the following day with more than 2,000 people in attendance. Crossing a rope more than 300ft in length and just 2½in thick, he used a balance pole to keep steady. During the same act he is reported to have done a somersault and handstand, all without falling from the great height. To finish his act he selected a member of the audience and took them across the rope on his back, no doubt to their tremendous anxiety.

Turning to pantomime after his tightrope retirement, Blondin continued performing up until 1896 when he was aged 71. He would die as a result of diabetes only a year later and is buried at Kensal Green Cemetery in London.

CHARACTERS

No matter where in the world you grow up there will always be local legends. From the odd man on the street who has numerous stories attached to him such as 'he won the lottery you know, but gave away all his winnings and chose to live a life of poverty', to 'he is that way because something dark happened to him in his past'. The truth is always elusive but here are some documented stories of our county's notables.

RUDOLF ABEL - THE GEORDIE SPY

Rudolf Abel was the alias used by a Soviet spy named William Genrikhovich Fisher, who was born in Benwell, Newcastle, on 11 July 1903. Often referred to as the most famous Soviet spy of all time, William's life would later become inspiration for Steven Spielberg's blockbuster *Bridge of Spies*.

Heinrich Fisher, William's father, had been a Bolshevik revolutionary and was a strong supporter of socialism. Heinrich had been imprisoned in his home country by the Tsarist authorities, which led him and his wife, Lyubov, to emigrate from Russia in 1901 by making their way across Germany. Upon arriving in Newcastle he got a job as an engine fitter at Armstrongs, where he worked for some time, while William studied at Monkseaton Grammar School. It is also believed that Heinrich was shipping guns from the North East to other Baltic states to help the proletariat.

The family then returned to Russia in 1921, where William would begin his career in the military before being sent to the USA to spy as part of the KGB. Throughout his career he assumed a number of identities, handling many agents, and was instrumental in getting information back to Russia. His cover was blown in 1957 and he was arrested, although he maintained the alias Rudolf Abel. William was spared the death penalty and was instead sentenced to thirty years in prison, of which he only served four after being exchanged for an American pilot.

No known recording of his voice exists so unfortunately it is difficult to establish if he spoke with a Geordie accent. William died in Moscow in 1971 and is often remembered as the spy who never broke.

TILLY TINMOUTH

Tilly Tinmouth is a Sunderland-born wrestler and women's weight-lifting champion of Great Britain. While there is little information about her younger years, some of her earliest appearances in newspapers came at the start of the 1930s. In 1932 it is reported the first women's weightlifting championships took place in Croydon, though Tilly Tinmouth is described as the current champion, and she came up against Miss Ivy Russell, whose occupation was a domestic servant. In reports for this bout it is stated that Tilly lived in the Millfield area of Sunderland. This clash of the titans saw Russell beat the northern champion by dead-lifting 300lb. Tilly continued exhibiting her strength at events up and down the country but reports suggest this was the end of her official competitive weightlifting.

However, this was far from the end of the Sunderland strong woman's career as she soon turned her talents elsewhere. The Imperial Troupe of Wrestlers came to the Theatre Royal in Sunderland, challenging any local women to step into the ring. Tilly accepted this challenge and impressed the troupe so much that she was immediately signed with them to go on tour. While she had wrestled previously as a hobby at a number of events, including St James Hall in Newcastle, which was reported to be the first event of its kind in the North, this was the start of her career as a wrestler.

Travelling with the troupe, she wrestled up and down the country, beating women from different parts of the world. On 9 January in 1933 she had a match against Miss Babs Thomas from Ireland, which she won. Another interesting match was one held at the Victoria Theatre in Dundee on 28 January. At this point she is described as the undefeated champion of the troupe, however a mysterious woman wearing a hooded mask was challenged to step in the ring. Tilly was defeated by the mystery athlete, who kept her identity secret as she described herself as a well-known athlete and swimmer whose parents disapproved of her wrestling.

Tilly's career as a wrestler saw her travel with the troupe to France and Belgium. Less than twenty years before her strength saw her skyrocketed to fame in the papers, women still did not have the right to vote, which makes Tilly's determination all the more impressive. While her amazing talent seems seldom remembered now she is definitely one woman who helped put Sunderland on the map.

LAMBERT'S LEAP

The story of Lambert's Leap begins more than 200 years ago in 1759. Cuthbert Lambert, the son of a local physician, was a customs officer who in this tale was riding on his horse attending to business. Many years ago in Heaton between Sandford Road and Portland Road there was once the wooded Sandyford Dene, which a bridge crossed over. In some versions of this story Lambert's horse was speeding towards the bridge and jumped the barrier, while in others the horse was spooked, which made it jump the barrier in shock. However, in all accounts Lambert went over the bridge along with his horse.

Beneath the bridge was no small drop, 37ft by some accounts, meaning Lambert was potentially staring death in the face. He is said to have grabbed the hanging branch of an old ash tree, saving himself from the terrible fall. His horse, however, was not so lucky and the fall proved fatal to his riding companion as it is reported the bones in its back were broken. The story of Lambert's miraculous survival was told nationwide and in commemoration of his luck the spot became known as Lambert's Leap.

Cuthbert Lambert would not be the only person to be forced over the bridge, however, as years later others would suffer the same fate. It is reported that on 18 August 1771 a servant of Lord Delaval was riding home when his horse became restless and also jumped the barrier. This time the rider was not lucky enough to grab a branch on his way down, however both the rider and his horse landed miraculously unhurt. On 5 December 1827 an apprentice to a local doctor with the surname Nicholson was visiting a patient in Long Benton. Reported to be a young man, Nicholson was riding at high speed over the bridge when again the horse leapt the barrier. On this occasion the rider was not so lucky and landed on sharp stones at the bottom of the ravine, dying on impact. It is said the town grieved for the loss of such a promising youth.

The dene was filled in shortly after this and Sandyford Burn is now believed to flow in a culvert below Grantham Road. The tale of Lambert's Leap was commemorated in a number of ways, including poems published at the time as well as a local pub named as such, which closed in 1971. While there is little to remind people of this local piece of folklore, the story of Cuthbert Lambert's lucky escape lives on.

THE DOCTOR

James Graham was a self-styled doctor and sexologist born in Scotland. Often dismissed as a quack for his unusual techniques by medical experts, he had total belief in his methods.

In July 1791, James came to Newcastle to showcase the nature and benefits of earth bathing to help cure diseases. He had himself and another young woman suffering from scorbutic disorder placed naked in a field and buried up to their lips in dirt in Hanover Square.

They remained there from 12 o'clock noon until 6 in the evening two days later.

Great numbers attended to see this curious exhibition, although the results remain a mystery.

FREEBORN JOHN

Believed to have been born in Sunderland in approximately 1614, John Lilburne is considered by some to be the first English radical. His father, Richard Lilburne, owned land in County Durham, allowing John to grow up in a fairly comfortable environment. Interestingly, Richard is thought to be the last man in England to have insisted that he should be allowed to settle a legal dispute by trial by combat. While he spent some of his youth in Greenwich, he returned to the North East in 1620, where he attended schools in Bishop Auckland and Newcastle.

On his return to London he became involved in the illegal printing and distribution of Puritan literature, for which he fled to Holland to avoid being charged. When he returned he was arrested in December 1637 and refused to take an oath or answer questions, insisting his arrest was unlawful. This would prolong his punishment and he was sentenced to be whipped, pilloried and imprisoned until he complied. In April 1638 he was whipped on the bare skin of his back with a three-pronged whip before being dragged to a pillory. This did not stop John campaigning though, and he continued trying to get his message out before he was gagged, then later thrown in prison.

He was imprisoned for three years before Oliver Cromwell drew attention to his case, seeing him released soon after. Upon gaining his freedom, John continued his campaigning for 'Freeborn Rights', which were defined as rights that every human is born with, not bestowed upon them by monarchy or government. These rights included the right to hear of what one was accused, the right to face one's accusers and the right to avoid self-incrimination. This early forerunner to human rights is considered one of the historical foundations for the Fifth Amendment featured in the United States Constitution.

With the outbreak of the first English Civil War, John sided with the Roundheads, supporting the Parliamentary side over the Royalists. He took part in numerous clashes and was eventually captured, despite jumping into the Thames in an effort to escape. This time he was part of a prisoner exchange that saw him released, but not before he was threatened with execution. Continuing to fight for his beliefs, he would see other battles and become friends with Cromwell, retiring from the army in April 1645.

Campaigning for what he believed in would see him imprisoned again in October 1645, this time for denouncing members of Parliament for living in comfort while the common man fought. Shortly after his imprisonment he was sent to the Tower of London and the demand for his freedom spawned the Leveller movement. Charged with high treason, he was exiled and travelled to the Netherlands but ultimately returned and showed support for the monarchy, providing the rights of the people were upheld. He was arrested again and sentenced to imprisonment, eventually being moved to Dover Castle, where he was allowed to see his family. Whilst visiting them in the summer of 1657, he caught a fever at Eltham in Kent and died.

BRAVERY IN THE FACE OF DANGER

Richard Wallace Annand was born in South Shields on 5 November 1914. Lieutenant Commander Wallace Moir Annand, Richard's father, would be killed in Gallipoli shortly after his birth in June 1915. After leaving school, Richard worked at the National Provincial Bank in South Shields and then left the North East to find work in other parts of the country. In 1933 he returned and joined the Royal Navy Volunteer reserves. He applied for a commission in 1937 but was rejected due to his age.

Instead, in 1938 he was commissioned into the Supplementary Reserve of Officers as a second lieutenant of the Durham Light Infantry. During the Second World War, while in Belgium in May 1940 near the River Dyle, Richard's brave actions would see him be the first member of the British Army to receive a Victoria Cross in the Second World War. Richard's platoon was on the south side of the river beside a destroyed bridge, which the platoon had been defending the night before. At 11 a.m. another attack was launched and an enemy bridging party was sent into the river to make repairs. Having run out of ammunition, Richard ran across the battlefield with total disregard for enemy mortar shells and gunfire until he reached the top of the bridge. From this position he inflicted more than twenty casualties with hand grenades and drove the invading party back.

Reunited with his platoon, he dressed his wounds and resumed command. The bridge continued to be attacked over the next twenty-four hours and Richard's skill with grenades undoubtedly helped hold back the enemy. While being attacked later that evening, his unit received the order to withdraw, but after learning that his batman had been wounded and left behind, Richard returned and brought him back in a wheelbarrow before he lost consciousness due to his injuries.

Richard was awarded the Victoria Cross, the highest and most prestigious award for gallantry in the face of the enemy that can be awarded to British and Commonwealth forces, by King George at Buckingham Palace in September 1940. He was later promoted to captain but soon retired due to disability, and began philanthropic work by becoming a founding member of the British Association for the Hard of Hearing and being involved in the founding of the Durham County Association for the Disabled. Richard died in December 2004 aged 90 and his service uniform and Victoria Cross are on display at the Durham Light Infantry Museum.

SPARKIE WILLIAMS

From Koko the Gorilla, who was proficient in sign language, to dogs riding skateboards on the internet, interesting characters do not always have to come in human form. Sparkie Williams is one such case. Living from 1954 to 1962, Sparkie was a world-famous talking budgie who became a celebrity after winning a speaking bird contest in 1958.

His vocabulary of more than 500 words and ability to recite eight nursery rhymes made him a sensation. He went on to perform on TV and radio, and even released a record that sold more than 20,000 copies.

After Sparkie's death he was stuffed and put on display at the Hancock Museum in Newcastle.

QUEEN OF THE DESERT

Gertrude Margaret Lowthian Bell was born in Washington New Hall, in what was then County Durham but is now Sunderland, on 14 July 1868. Sir Isaac Lowthian Bell, Gertrude's father, was a prominent iron master and politician, which likely exposed Gertrude to international matters and spurred her curiosity for the world at a young age. She moved to London and studied history – one of the few subjects women were allowed to study at the time – at Queen's College, then attended an Oxford University to earn a first-class honours degree in Modern History.

Shortly after graduating, Gertrude visited her uncle in Tehran, Persia, where he was employed in a role similar to that of a British ambassador. Gertrude then spent the next decade travelling the world, becoming fluent in Arabic, Persian, French and German as well as speaking Italian and Turkish. She developed a love of the Middle East and through her writing and photographs helped expose its beauty to the world. Her intimate knowledge of the countries and their tribes made her a target for British Intelligence recruitment during the First World War, during which she worked with Lawrence of Arabia and heavily influenced Winston Churchill's decision-making in the Middle East.

At the end of the war, during the dismantling of the Ottoman Empire, Gertrude focused on the creation of Iraq and its first king becoming a powerful force in Iraqi politics. She went on to found the Baghdad Archaeological Museum but after frequent health issues died later that year. At a time when women in Britain were fighting for the vote, Gertrude's passion for the Middle East provided invaluable knowledge and insight into an area of the world that is still considered complicated today.

Her story has been popularised by a film directed by Werner Herzog that was released in 2015 titled *Queen of the Desert*. A more in-depth look at her life is the documentary *Letters from Baghdad*, which contains archival footage and insight.

TITO'S GUESTS

During 1953, Yugoslavian leader Josip Broz Tito paid a visit to the UK, where he met the Queen and Winston Churchill. Initially created after the First World War, it was not until 1929 that the country would first be named the Kingdom of Yugoslavia. After the Second World War, Yugoslavia was set up as a federation of six republics with borders drawn along ethnic and historical lines: Bosnia and Herzegovina, Croatia, Macedonia, Montenegro, Serbia and Slovenia.

After visiting the UK, Tito returned to Yugoslavia, where he wrote to Churchill inviting twenty children whose fathers had been killed in Yugoslavia during the war for a holiday as a small repayment. Three of those invited were children from the North East: Ivor Sword, aged 11, and his sister June, 10, of West Road, Denton Square, and Robert Wilson, 14, of Weardale Avenue, Blyth.

The children spent an August in Yugoslavia and were given 1,000 dinars a week pocket money, with the rest of the costs paid for by the government. All the children reportedly enjoyed their holiday and were pleased at having met Marshal Tito in person. June, who was the youngest girl in the party, was invited back to Yugoslavia with her friends, although it is not known if she returned.

Regarded as a revolutionary by some and a dictator by others, Tito's kind gesture to three North East children now seems to have been forgotten. After his death in 1980 political crisis led to heavy conflict in the country, and in the 1990s many of the republics declared independence, breaking up Yugoslavia.

RACEWALKER

Born in Newcastle in 1766 to Robert Wilson, a shipbuilder, and Mary Finlay, George Wilson became infamous for his long walks. Following his father's death, the family was left with a large debt and his mother turned to being a pawnbroker to pay off the sum.

Throughout his life George was employed in various jobs, serving as a clerk at his mother's business, as an apprentice cobbler, and he even started his own business. While working as a hosier and draper he was required to travel to London, a journey that is reported to have seen him cross more than 500 miles, which he always travelled on foot. During this time, he was also employed as a tax collector and would regularly walk 50 to 60 miles a day fulfilling his duties.

Upon returning to Newcastle, following a small period of work in London, he began looking for wagers on walking long distances. It is thought the first wager he took part in was to complete the 84-mile walk along the length of Hadrian's Wall within twenty-four hours. Due to small debts he ended up in debtors' prison on more than one occasion but even then he continued wagering on distances he could cross in a set time.

As George's reputation grew so did the challenges placed before him, with perhaps the most famous being offered £100 to walk 1,000 miles around Blackheath Common in Surrey within twenty days in 1815. Averaging about 50 miles a day at 4mph, George was not allowed to walk on the Sabbath and his initial venture did not receive much attention. By the ninth day, following reports in the press, a crowd of more than 7,000 had gathered to watch him walk and the dust created began to impair his breathing.

George's determination to complete the challenge disgruntled a number of those who had bets on him and more than one attempt was made to stop him. The local authorities had become annoyed at the attention the feat was receiving as the crowd attracted drinking, circus acts and prostitution, with concerns that the situation may lead to a riot. Before he could finish the challenge, he was arrested for disturbing the peace. Although he was acquitted, the disruption resulted in failure and the crowd dispersed upon news of the warrant spreading.

This event earned him the title 'the Blackheath Pedestrian', by which he is now commonly known. A year later, in 1816, he completed 1,000 miles of walking within twenty-four hours in Hull, finally fulfilling his goal. George Wilson lived to the age of 73, passing away following a short illness in Pandon Dean, Newcastle.

DOLLY PEEL

Dolly Peel was a famous Victorian character in South Shields. Thought to have been born in 1782, Dolly was a fishwife, smuggler and protector of local sailors from the press gangs.

Dolly's husband, Cuthbert, and her son were both press-ganged to serve in the Royal Navy during Britain's wars with America and France. Dolly sneaked aboard the ship with them and hid until she was discovered and made to work as a nurse to sick and injured sailors. Her work earned her a great deal of respect and she was allowed to stay aboard the ship with her family. Upon their release, Dolly was pardoned while her husband and son were made exempt from future press-ganging.

Back home, Dolly became a local legend known for her wit and interesting stories. As well as selling contraband goods, she published poetry and helped shelter sailors from suffering the same fate forced on her family.

In 1987 a statue was erected in South Shields depicting Dolly looking out across the Tyne, and it is intended as a tribute to the strength of local women.

RECOGNITION

Did you know that in 1967 Martin Luther King Jr, leader of the American Civil Rights Movement, visited Newcastle?

Dr King was awarded an honorary degree of Doctor of Civil Law by Newcastle upon Tyne University and visited the North East to collect it, where he gave a speech. Following this he states, 'It may be true that the law cannot make a man love me … but it can restrain him from lynching me.'

Sadly Dr King was assassinated only a year later on 4 April 1968.

In 1987, world-renowned physicist Stephen Hawking was also honoured by Newcastle University. Visiting the North East a year before publishing his book *A Brief History of Time*, he received an

honorary Doctor of Sciences Degree. Undoubtedly one of the greatest minds the world has known, Hawking passed away in March 2018.

THE HERO OF CAMPERDOWN

Jack Crawford (22 March 1775–10 November 1831) was a sailor of the Royal Navy known as the 'Hero of Camperdown'. Born in the east end of Sunderland, Jack started his career at sea aged 12 after joining the crew of the *Peggy* in South Shields as an apprentice.

The Battle of Camperdown took place during 1797 between the British North Sea Fleet and the Dutch Navy, and is regarded as the most significant action between the British and Dutch forces during the French Revolutionary Wars.

Jack was a crew member aboard the *Venerable*, Admiral Duncan's flagship, during the battle. During the exchange of fire a shell took off part of the mast, causing the flag to fall to the deck. The importance of having the flag raised was paramount as lowering it signalled for the rest of the fleet to cease fire and withdraw. Despite the intense gunfire, Jack climbed up what was left of the mast and nailed down the flag. The Dutch fleet was annihilated and Jack was regarded as a hero for his actions upon his return and recognised by the King for his valiant efforts.

However, in later years Jack fell on hard times and turned to alcohol, frequently pawning his medals. He became the second recorded fatality of the cholera epidemic in Sunderland and died on 10 November 1831, being buried in an unmarked pauper's grave.

A statue was erected in Mowbray Park in 1890 in memory of his brave actions and still stands there today.

ADMIRAL LORD COLLINGWOOD

Another hero from the French Revolutionary period is Cuthbert Collingwood, who was born in Newcastle in September 1748.

Attending Newcastle Royal Grammar School before his career at sea began at the age of 12, Collingwood would spend forty-four years of his life away at sea. In 1774 he sailed to Boston, where he fought as part of the British Naval Brigade at the Battle of Bunker Hill, which was part of the early stages of the American Revolutionary War. Following his actions there he was commissioned as lieutenant and he began building on an already sturdy career at sea.

Shortly after this he served with Horatio Nelson and they rose to the rank of post-captain together, which would be the start of a lifelong friendship. He then began taking command of ships and spent a great deal of time in the West Indies stopping American ships from trading there. Following his service there he made one of his few return trips home and married Sarah Blackett, the daughter of the Mayor of Newcastle, with whom he had two daughters.

The ramifications of the French Revolution were felt around the world and Collingwood returned to serving his country the best way he knew how. His skills saw him serve at some of the most famous battles of this period, such as the Glorious First of June in 1794 and the Battle of Cape St Vincent in 1797. Arguably his most notable effort would occur at the Battle of Trafalgar, an event that is considered by some to be one of British history's most important.

In October 1805, the combined strength of the French and Spanish navies were set to clash with British forces. The British Fleet had been split into two columns, one under the command of Horatio Nelson, the other under Collingwood. The bloody battle that ensued would see many heroes but after the fatal wounding of Nelson it was a man from the North East who stepped up to save the nation. As Nelson lay dying, Collingwood defeated the foreign forces and thus cemented Nelson's place in history.

Following his brave actions on that day, despite wanting to return to his home in Morpeth with his family, he continued serving in the Mediterranean. It would be 1810 before he was finally granted permission to return to his beloved North East but he unfortunately died from cancer while making the journey. He is buried alongside his close friend Nelson in the crypt of St Paul's Cathedral in London.

If the Battle of Trafalgar had been lost, Napoleon's forces were set to invade England and the course of history would have been changed forever. Cuthbert Collingwood is an often forgotten local hero but without his endeavours I am sure our lives would be very different today. He is commemorated through a number of local and international places named after him as well as through a large monument that overlooks the River Tyne in Tynemouth.

HARD TIMES FOR JEM MACE

Born in Beeston in Norfolk in 1831, James 'The Gypsy' Mace was an English boxing champion. Debuting in 1857 in bare-knuckle fights and holding the title of 'Champion of England' by 1861, Jem Mace was a middleweight known for out-boxing heavier opponents using his dancing style, clever defensive tactics and powerful, accurate punching.

Bare-knuckle boxing was an outlawed sport and as such Mace was liable to arrest. On the night before defending his title in 1867 he was bound in court and ordered not to fight again. Considered by some as the father of modern boxing, he then travelled to the US, where he gave exhibitions of gloved boxing before an attempt on his life in Mississippi led him to return to England. In 1876 he returned to America as a gloved boxer, before moving on to Australia to pave the way for gloved boxing as a professional sport.

Travelling the world at a time when most would barely leave their city, Jem Mace accrued a fortune buying hotels in different parts of the world, racehorses, and even a circus at one point. Unfortunately, his biggest vice was gambling and as the years went on his wealth gradually disappeared.

His misfortune would take him to Jarrow, where in 1910 he was busking on the streets with his violin. It was here that the once great champion would die penniless. His body was sent to Liverpool and buried in an unmarked grave in Anfield Cemetery. In 2002, the Merseyside Former Boxers Association arranged a memorial headstone by his grave.

THE GREATEST LIAR ON EARTH

It was 1898 when the world first heard of Louis de Rougemont and his amazing adventures. *Wide World Magazine* was first to publish his alleged exploits, all of which if true would cement his place in history as one of the great explorers of his time. Being the sole survivor of a shipwreck, he was first said to have landed on an island before travelling across Australia.

Following a brief publication in the mentioned magazine, he wrote a book that detailed stories of his adventures titled *The Adventures of Louis de Rougemont*. This contained tales of giant octopus, his fights with crocodiles and interactions with native tribes. He states in the book that he was taken in by a tribe and worshipped like a god – something that is still parodied in castaway scenes today – fathering a child and leading the tribe into battle. One extraordinary story even had a local connection to Sunderland.

In one exploit de Rougemont tells how he saved two Sunderland girls named Blanche and Gladys Rogers, who had been shipwrecked, from a tribe of cannibals. Once he had saved them, however, a shot from a passing ship killed them, leaving no evidence to back up his claim. While some believed his fantastical story, it did not take long for those who were suspicious to begin investigating. The *Sunderland Echo*, intrigued by his claims, began speaking to local people to find evidence that the deceased captain of the ship or his two daughters ever existed and published their results in September 1898. A number of people were interviewed about their memories of ships and their captains, none of whom could remember such people existing. This was not the only claim to be proven false and things quickly unravelled for de Rougemont.

It soon transpired that the man claiming to be de Rougemont was in fact named Henri Louis Grin. Born in 1847 in Switzerland, Henri had worked in a number of jobs and travelled somewhat before making his sensational and untrue claims. His real wife from many years earlier came forward to refute the stories he had told, arguably putting the final nail in his coffin. Interestingly, one story he told was proved credible as he had previously described riding a giant sea turtle. This was tested in

London, where before a crowd of people he climbed onto the back of a turtle in the water and rode it.

Once Henri had been exposed as a fraud he toured parts of South Africa and Australia, performing as 'the Greatest Liar on Earth' but was often booed off stage. Shortly after this he disappeared from the spotlight and is believed to have died penniless in London in 1921.

'Truth is stranger than fiction. But De Rougemont is stranger than both.'

Wide World Magazine, June 1899, No. 14

THE MAN WHO SOLD COALS TO NEWCASTLE

Timothy Dexter was born in 1747 in Malden, Massachusetts, into a family of colonial farmers who struggled to make ends meet. At the age of 8 he dropped out of school to work as a farm labourer but, determined to make something of himself, he became an apprentice leather dresser at the age of 16 and in 1769 moved to Newburyport to start his own business.

It was through his business that he met Elizabeth Frothingham, a wealthy widow who owned an established leather shop. The two soon married and Dexter moved with her to her large estate in Boston. His aspirations did not stop there, however, and his entrepreneurial spirit led him to seek counsel from others he deemed to have similar social status. Timothy was considered by many of his snobby peers to be an illiterate fraud and he was disliked by the elite community in Boston.

In an attempt to bankrupt Timothy, he was advised to invest in continental currency, which was worthless at the time. However, after the American Revolutionary War, the US government made good on the dollars and he amassed a fortune. He took this and began an export trade to the West Indies, where his colleagues advised him – again maliciously – to send bed warming pans, used to heat cold beds in winter. However, these ended up being sold as cooking pans at a high price.

Due to him being largely uneducated it seems Timothy acted on the bad advice time and time again. An idiom that is still used around the world today is 'Like coals to Newcastle' and it is often used to refer to a pointless action. The first use of this phrase can be traced back to 1679, so by the time Dexter was jokingly advised to send coal to Newcastle many thought he would not take it seriously. When he did send the coal to Newcastle it was at a time during which the miners were striking, and its delivery saw him receive a price, nonetheless.

His reputation as an eccentric was increased by him telling people his wife was deceased when she was not, and that people who saw her in the windows were seeing her ghost. In perhaps his most famous moment, he faked his own death and watched in secret to see how people would react. Enraged at not seeing his wife cry, Timothy later revealed the hoax and caned her. Shortly after this bizarre episode, Timothy Dexter died a second time in 1806 and this time it was permanent.

COFFEE JOHNNY

John Oliver, also known as Coffee Johnny, was born in Winlaton, Gateshead, in 1829. Though little is known about the early years of his life, Coffee Johnny's fighting skills soon earned him a reputation as more than just a blacksmith. At a time when bare-knuckle boxing had no rules, fights would often go on until one opponent could no longer stand.

On 27 May 1850, Coffee Johnny fought Will Renwick, who had a reputation as a pugilist and a man of violence. The fight lasted thirty-six rounds and went on for one hour and ten minutes. Renwick was taken home in a cart once the fight was over to be tended to by the doctor. Joe Oliver, Coffee Johnny's grandson, recalls the tale of a fight with the landlord of a pub at Tanfield, with the surname Kirsopp:

When he fit Kirsopp at Tanfield, Coffee won. The landlord paid him as the loser of the fight. And from that day on Kirsopp walked with his head tilted to one side till the day he died. Coffee must have hit him bloody hard.

Coffee Johnny became a local celebrity and was easily recognised by his tall stature and white top hat. Aside from boxing, Johnny was also a keen hunter and was interested in racing. Known to have a sense of humour, one story tells how while he was out hunting with Lord Ravensworth he made the following joke: 'I will be a bigger landowner than you some day,' Coffee told Lord Ravensworth.

'How's that?' Ravensworth replied.

'Because when I die it will take seven foot of land to bury me but less to bury you, so I'll be a bigger landowner.'

John Oliver would also become immortalised in the Geordie folk song 'Blaydon Races', cementing his place in local folklore. John died in April 1900 and was buried in St Paul's in Winlaton. As he predicted, his burial plot is over 7ft, the biggest in the churchyard.

GIANT'S FUNERAL

William Campbell was a Scottish man born in 1856 who claimed to be the heaviest in the world. Weighing upwards of 40st in his teenage years, William's weight increased over time and it is thought he weighed 52st at the end of his life. Born in a Glasgow slum, he went on to be part of a freak show and was exhibited in full highland dress at the Egyptian Hall in London.

William and his wife, Polly, took up the lease of the Duke of Wellington pub in Newcastle in 1877. Due to William's large size and health problems most of the responsibility fell on Polly; however, his time owning the pub was short-lived and he fell seriously ill a few months later and died.

An upstairs window and part of the wall had to be removed to allow his large coffin to be hoisted up to his room, where a group of strong men heaved the corpse in. A trolley was used to transport the body to a hearse. The unusual size of the man had attracted masses of spectators desperate to catch a view of the unique sight, with some even climbing Grey's Monument. William was buried in Jesmond cemetery, with more than 2,000 people in attendance.

Due to William never having been officially weighed, his title of world's heaviest man was forgotten soon after his death.

A CONFLICT WITH PIRATES

Richard Avery Hornsby, of Vine Street, Sunderland, was the captain of the merchant ship *Wrightson and Isabella*. His ship engaged in trade across the North Sea and had a crew of just five men and three boys, all from Sunderland. The ship itself was built for speed rather than battle but still carried four small guns, two swivel cannons and a few blunderbusses.

In 1744, during a routine trip carrying malt and barley, the ship encountered another ship known as *Marquis of Brances*, which was manned by seventy-five French pirates. The *Marquis of Brances* outmanned and outgunned the much smaller merchant ship but would prove no match against Hornsby and his crew. Twice the pirate ship tried to board the *Isabella* and twice the captain managed to fend off the attacks. At one point the captain of the pirate ship shouted over to Hornsby: 'Strike you English dog.' To which the captain replied: 'Come aboard if you dare.'

The fighting raged on for hours, with both sides continuously spraying the other with bullets and shrapnel. Captain Hornsby, believing the pirate ship was now fleeing, let out a round of three cheers with his crew before the attacking ship targeted them once more. Hornsby received an injury to the temple and was bleeding profusely during the carnage. This time when the pirate ship was close enough to board the crew were too scared to jump on, having previously been met with the defensive ferocity the small British ship had to offer. The pirates had no other choice but to flee – however, after only a short distance the ship exploded and sank, leaving only three survivors of its crew of seventy-five.

Upon his return to England, Captain Hornsby was awarded a gold medal and chain by King George II at a ceremony in Kensington Palace in September 1744. Each of the men were given a bounty of £5, while the boys received 40s each.

TESTO'S ROUNDABOUT

Testo's roundabout is a junction of the A19 in Sunderland. While many people will have passed this junction and heard its name, few will know why it is so named.

The Testo family first came to England in the 1700s from France, where Felix Testo was a well-known performer and conjurer. His descendants continued the tradition, constantly changing their acts to include new and exciting ways to capture the audience. Some of the feats performed were called 'the dancing and speaking monkey' and 'Transformation of a bird to a child growing into a lady'.

In 1906 the Testos presented the first films to be shown in Newcastle, including titles such as *Lens Colliery Disaster*, *The Life of Charles Peace* and *Too Late to Turn Back*. The family and their world-famous flea circus also became a regular fixture at the Hoppings Fair.

At the location of the roundabout once stood a garage and car dealership owned by Britain's most famous flea circus ringmaster, Alfred Testo. Supplies of fleas dropped dramatically in England as hygiene improved, and flea circuses are now rarely seen.

WANDERING WILLIE

The tale of Wandering Willie is a sad one and is tied to the loyalty of a dog who became somewhat of a legend in his local area. Believed to have been first recorded by Thomas Hudson in the *Monthly Chronicle of North County Lore and Legend* in 1889, the story of Willie begins a few years earlier.

While transporting a flock of sheep from the Cheviots in Northumberland to the Cleveland Hills, via the Shields Ferry, the farmer in command was dismayed to see his sheep scatter due to being startled by the bustling city life. Willie his loyal dog began pursuing the livestock and rounding them up, until only one was eventually found to be missing. Away the dog went, only for the missing sheep to be found before he returned, and after some time waiting the farmer moved on. When the dog returned from his search for the missing livestock the sun had set and he found himself alone.

For a considerable period of time Willie is said to have accepted no food from strangers, living only on scraps and growling at those who tried to show him kindness, because of his loyalty to his former master. As he began withering away some men decided to put him out of his misery, in what was considered a humane way at the time, throwing him overboard from a steam ferry. His fierce desire to live saw him survive the incident and despite the crashing waves he made it to shore. Willie resumed his search shortly after and would travel the ferry journey over and over in hopes of finding his owner once more.

His master did return the following autumn having heard about his pet's woes, but reportedly missed Willie by only a few minutes and was unable to recover him on that journey. As time passed he grew less wary of strangers and became the subject of sympathy for the many locals who knew his story. He is said to have been the first one off the ferry, barking as if to let everyone know he had safely brought its passengers over the water.

In 1880 Willie sadly passed away from old age after many years of searching for his master and surviving on the kindness of strangers. Ralph the ferryman, who had grown close to him, had the loyal dog stuffed. He was then mounted in a glass case and put in the Turks Head Pub in Tynemouth, where he remains on display to this day.

SECRET LIFE BY THE WEAR

The Battle of Culloden took place in April 1746 and is considered the last major confrontation in the Jacobite uprising. On Culloden Moor, Scottish clansmen fought against the British Army, resulting in their brutal defeat and caused those who had rebelled to retreat. One of those involved was James Drummond, Earl of Perth, and while a number of those caught retreating were charged with treason and beheaded, he escaped.

Fleeing on horseback, James made it to a safe location and went into hiding. It is thought that after a number of weeks he boarded a ship taking him to the North East under a false identity, where he eventually made it to Sunderland. From here he moved on to South Biddick and began living a new life in exile by the banks of the River Wear. It is thought by some that it was James himself who began circulating a rumour that he had died while on a ship to France with his brother in an effort to throw his pursuers off his scent.

James settled into his new life and began courting Elizabeth Armstrong, the daughter of his landlord, eventually marrying her in 1749. He is said to have kept his previous life of nobility a secret from his wife until his second son announced his wish to become a miner. Hopes of returning to his home and claiming what was rightfully his were destroyed when a flood washed away the boathouse he had been working in, taking with it an old wooden chest filled with the documents needed to prove his claim. Legend has it he walked the banks of the River Wear on many a day looking to find the wooden chest without success. James returned home in secret on a number of occasions, however he did not manage to reclaim his estate before his death in 1782.

The story could well have ended there, however his sons then took on the responsibility of the claim and began fighting to inherit their father's land. His first son was thought to have come very close, but he died at sea when his ship sank, taking the entire crew with it. Thomas Drummond, James' grandson, took up the crusade next. Thought to have had a drinking problem, his claim was hampered by his lack of sobriety and despite being recognised by some it too went unfulfilled. The estates were eventually claimed by the Duke of Melfort and with it the dreams of the Wearside Drummonds were extinguished.

James Drummond, the fugitive earl, is buried in a churchyard near Penshaw, as is his grandson, Thomas. The last record of him in the church register is as follows:'Thomas Drummond, Alleged Earl of Perth, buried November 22, 1873. 81 years. Signed Philip Thompson (rector).'

NAMING THE NEANDERTHAL

William King was born in Sunderland in 1809 to parents William King and Eleanor née Armstrong. King's father was a coal worker while his

mother was a confectioner and shop owner. During his early years he studied in Sunderland before trying his hand at becoming an apprentice in a variety of trades such as ironmonger, bookseller and librarian. King went on to become secretary and librarian of the Sunderland Literary and Philosophical Society, and then in 1840 was offered the position of curator for Newcastle Museum, which he accepted.

William did not come from a particularly wealthy background and while employed there he supplemented his income by dealing in fossils and minerals. This became an issue for the museum committee, whose attention was drawn to King's personal collection, which contained valuable specimens that had not been offered to the museum. When told he could no longer deal or collect on his own while employed as curator he defied the restriction and was dismissed. King, however, did not wish to leave his post and refused to give up the keys, forcing the museum to change its locks.

In 1849 he joined Queens College in Galway as its first Professor of Geology and it was here he made his biggest impact. In 1864 he published *The reputed fossil man of the Neanderthal*, based on the cast of the top of a skull from the Neander Valley in Germany. This revolutionary paper is arguably a huge moment in the history of the study of evolution, as it was the first time a scientist had looked at a fossil thinking that while it appeared human it was also a distinctly different species. Supporting a modified theory of Darwin's *Origin of Species*, which had been published in 1859, King believed the Neanderthal to have little in the way of intelligence and mental faculties.

While the Neanderthal still remains the most well-known sub-species of human, the man who named it is now largely forgotten. After he published his theory he continued teaching until 1883, when he had a stroke and resigned. William King died at Glenoir, Galway, on 24 June 1886.

MUTINY ON HMS *BOUNTY*

The story of the mutiny that took place on board HMS *Bounty* in 1789 is one that has been told and retold on and off screen numerous times since the events took place more than 200 years ago. The *Bounty* was a Royal Navy vessel that left England in 1787 and was tasked with collecting and transporting breadfruit plants from Tahiti to the West Indies. While performing its duty the ship had a five-month layover in Tahiti, where many of the crew lived ashore and formed relationships with native Polynesian women. Relationships between the captain, Lieutenant William Bligh, and his crew quickly deteriorated when he began handing out harsh punishments and being abusive to his men. Fletcher Christian, the master's mate on board the ship, was said to be a particular target of this abuse.

After three weeks back at sea, Christian and a number of men on board seized the captain and others loyal to him and threatened them with execution if they did not co-operate. Captain Bligh tried to reason with the men, reportedly speaking to some by name, demanding to be set free. This did not work, however, and Bligh, along with those loyal to him, were forced on board a small ship and cast out to sea. One of those men was named Thomas McIntosh, who was from North Shields. McIntosh was brought back on board the *Bounty* because of his skills as a carpenter and in part because the ship soon to be cast away was already too full.

McIntosh was 26 years old when he first joined the crew of the *Bounty* and is described by Captain Bligh at the time of the mutiny as being '28 years, 5 feet 6 inches high. Fair complexion, light-brown hair, slender made. Pitted by smallpox'. McIntosh was said to have formed a relationship with a woman in Tahiti, whom he called Mary. When the crew arrived in Tubai they were attacked by a native war party, who suffered great casualties in their attempt to stop the invaders. Fletcher realised for the settlement to be a success he needed compliant men and women and so the *Bounty* returned to Tahiti briefly, bringing back natives, many of whom had been deceived about the true reasons for the voyage. For the next two months Fletcher and his men tried unsuccessfully to make Tubai their new home but because of persistent clashes with tribes he was forced to call a vote, in which many of the crew voted to return to Tahiti. Mary had followed McIntosh to Tubai and remained loyal to the man who became a pirate against his will.

Their return to Tahiti was an unwelcome one as the people there had learned of their lies from the crew of a passing British ship. Fearing violence, Fletcher left with the few hardcore mutineers loyal to him, leaving McIntosh and many others in Tahiti.

Captain Bligh and his overcrowded boat of castaways initially landed on the nearby island of Tofua, but after a clash with natives there in which one of the crew was stoned to death, the crew decided to make the long and difficult journey to Timor, roughly 4,000 miles away. This journey would test the men with other stops on dangerous islands and relationships being pushed to breaking point, but while there were some casualties the crew eventually made it to their destination. Once the authorities were informed of the mutiny, HMS *Pandora* was dispatched to Tahiti in 1790 to capture the *Bounty* and force its crew to stand trial.

When the *Pandora* arrived in Tahiti, McIntosh was said to be the only loyalist to flee to the mountains to hide with the mutineers. Some believe this was because of the close relationship he had formed with Mary, who he knew he would be forced to leave. Those on Tahiti, including McIntosh, were captured and put in a specially designed prison on board the *Pandora* dubbed Pandora's Box. This prison would prove deadly, however, when the ship ran aground in the outer Great

Barrier Reef and many of those inside it drowned. McIntosh was one of the survivors and after another dangerous journey to safety was transported back to England to stand trial. His loyalty to Bligh saw him acquitted of charges, while those found guilty were sentenced to death by hanging. He returned to North Shields, where little is known about his life afterwards.

Captain Bligh returned to Tahiti on a second breadfruit expedition, where he encountered Mary McIntosh. Mary showed him a little girl who was said to be the daughter of Thomas, named Elizabeth. Whether Bligh informed Thomas of his daughter now thousands of miles away is unknown but from the information we have on him this does seem unlikely.

As for Fletcher Christian and the remaining mutineers, they settled on Pitcairn Island, burning the *Bounty* to hide the evidence. It was here tensions eventually rose between the Tahitians and the Europeans, resulting in the murder of Christian, who was shot and bludgeoned to death with an axe. The violence between the Tahitians and among the mutineers themselves would see all killed but one named Adams, who lived on the island and created a thriving civilisation that remained undiscovered until 1808. When the news eventually reached Britain, no action was taken against Adams and he remained there until his death in 1829.

LIEUTENANT COLONEL ERNEST VAUX

Born in 1865, Ernest Vaux was a member of the Vaux Breweries family, which was established as Vaux Breweries by Ernest's grandfather, Cuthbert Vaux, in 1806. Ernest was educated at Worcester College for the Blind Sons of Gentlemen and went on to join the Durham Royal Garrison Artillery volunteers.

During the Second Boer War in South Africa, Ernest volunteered for service and he commanded the Maxim Guns, taking part in more than eighty operations. It was his safe return from the war that prompted the family brewery to introduce the Double Maxim brand in 1901, a beer that continues to be brewed today. The outbreak of the First World War lead to Ernest returning to the battlefield and the 7th Battalion, Durham Light Infantry, of which he was commander, saw some of the bloodiest action on the Western Front. One particular story of his bravery tells how while holding a trench the men were attacked with gas. Vaux ordered his men to get out of the trench and stand up so as to avoid the low-hanging gas cloud and sing a hymn with him. This helped buy enough time for reinforcements to arrive and maintain their position. Vaux was reported to be a very respected and popular commander, often leading by example.

Ernest met Robert Baden-Powell in South Africa and the two became close friends. Upon his return to England he began taking the sons of his brewery workers and other Sunderland boys on camping weekends. In 1908, Lord Baden-Powell visited him in Sunderland and together they created what is considered by many to be the world's first official Scout group, named the Vaux Own.

While at a dinner party in 1925, Vaux choked on a rabbit bone. Medical assistance was not provided quickly enough and while his life was saved his health was so severely affected he had to be moved to a nursing home for treatment. Lieutenant Colonel Ernest Vaux died in 1925 aged 60 and was buried in Barton, North Yorkshire.

BREAKING THE LAW

Lawbreaking can come in many forms and varying degrees of seriousness. Crimes worthy of corporal punishment in the past are now often dealt with in very different ways. The fascination remains, nonetheless, with those who commit these acts in all their forms, as seen by the rising popularity of documentaries giving insight into the minds of criminals. Below are just a few tales of crimes in Tyne and Wear that caught the attention of the public and some that have now slipped away into the depths of history.

BODYSNATCHING - NEWCASTLE, 1825

In 1832 the Anatomy Act was passed in parliament, allowing freer license to medical professionals to dissect bodies. Prior to this, under the Murder Act of 1752 only the bodies of executed murderers were allowed to be used for dissection. This method did not provide enough subjects for the high demand of bodies to dissect and grave robbing became a frequent occurrence.

The Turf Hotel in Newcastle was a popular coaching inn and stop for goods travelling up and down the country, which became notorious for its relationship with the grim trade of selling the dead. On the evening of 1 September 1825, a trunk was dropped off to be delivered in Edinburgh the following morning. Due to the trunk being misplaced it remained in the hotel office for a number of days, when a foul smell began to circulate. This soon caught the attention of the staff, who noticed a liquid oozing from the package and immediately notified the police. Inside was the body of a teenage girl.

The police tracked down the man who dropped off the container but he was soon let go due to lack of evidence. It was reported, however, that a week after his being released a timber merchant came forward saying he recognised the man as having bought timber from him prior to the discovery.

The discovery of bodies at the Turf Hotel became so frequent that when a suspicious package arrived staff would often turn it away and send it back to where it came from. Legend has it that the porters of the hotel became so tired of this they took matters into their own hands and dumped the bodies in the Tyne.

BUTCH CASSIDY

You have probably heard of Butch Cassidy, one of America's most infamous outlaws. But did you know about his connection to the North East?

Robert Leroy Parker was born in North America, Utah in 1866. His parents Maximilian Parker and Sarah Giles, however, were born right here in the North East in Newcastle in 1849. Ann, the daughter of Robert Giles and Jane Sinclair, was from Stirlingshire but by the 1840s they had moved up to Newcastle.

The Census record states clearly where the three Giles children were born with John Giles being born in Scotland in 1846 but Ann and her younger brother were both born in Newcastle in 1849 and 1850.

The family lived on Tyneside for almost a decade before picking up sticks and moving to New York by 1856. From here they travelled to Utah where Ann met her future husband Maximilian. Their first son Robert (the infamous Butch Cassidy) was born on April 13 1866 a year after they were married.

He would later go on to rob trains and banks before escaping to South America, where he was allegedly killed in a shootout on 7 November 1908 aged 42.

TREASON IN TUDOR TIMES

Buried deep in the State Papers Foreign and Domestic of Henry VIII is a letter containing the story of how the unsuspecting actions of a local priest and fishermen led to their own execution. Henry VIII was King of England from 1509 to 1547 and is perhaps best known for his many wives. Following the revolt of 1536, known as the Pilgrimage of Grace, Henry brutally put down the rebellion by luring its leader to a location under terms of safe conduct, then hanging him and his men.

During the revolt James V, King of Scotland, had travelled to France to wed the daughter of the French monarch, who was in ill health. James had hoped to travel overland due to the frailty of his wife but Henry refused the request, seeing James as a potential rival to the throne. It was this that led James to travel via boat and on his return, while dropping anchor at Scarborough, a group of boats pulled up alongside his ship and implored him to invade. Surprised by the demand and eager to get his new bride home he continued north, where he would drop anchor again, this time in Whitburn.

Again a group of fishermen pulled up alongside the docked boat to implore King James to help. This time a party from the ship came ashore, most likely in search of food, and listened to the local men. One member of King James' crew was an Englishman in French service named James Crane. Unbeknownst to anyone aboard the ship, Crane was a spy for Henry's most loyal follower, Thomas Cromwell. Crane proceeded to speak with Robert Hodge, the priest of Whitburn Parish, in detail about his grievances. Hodge then described the sad state of affairs in England and even went as far as saying he wanted to see Cromwell hanged.

Hodge had chosen the wrong person to confide in as, shortly after, he and two other mariners believed to have been present were executed and hung in chains in Newcastle in September of 1537. Henry VIII's paranoia would eventually lead him to execute even his most loyal follower Cromwell under what he would later consider ill advice from his council.

THE MURDER OF NICHOLAS FAIRLES

On 2 June 1832, two Jarrow pitmen had been drinking in the now long-demolished pub named The Gaslight. William Jobling and Ralph Armstrong were both on strike and had been drinking before heading home. On their walk home they encountered Nicholas Fairles, a local magistrate and Justice of the Peace, and attempted to beg him for money.

Fairles refused to hand over any money and was almost beaten to death with sticks and stones. The local magistrate survived long enough to indicate that it was Armstrong who had unleashed the unplanned attack on him and not Jobling. Both of the men had escaped the scene of the crime but Jobling was quickly captured on a beach at South Shields, while Armstrong allegedly escaped overseas.

Jobling was tried for murder in Durham, being found guilty and sentenced to hang. After the execution had taken place Jobling's body was taken and put in an iron frame and displayed in sight of his widow's house for all to see. The body was left to decay for a number of weeks before it disappeared in the dead of night, when some say his family took it down and buried it in secret.

Jobling was one of the last people in the United Kingdom to be gibbeted. Many considered Jobling to be a martyr, questioning if his punishment was for murder or for being a part of the rebellious working class of the era.

THE FLYING BUTCHER

As reported on the Gateshead County Police's website:

On the night of Wednesday, 16th January, 1889, PC Graham was on duty in High Street, Wrekenton when he was called to Wilkinson's house where the 'Flying Butcher' was in the process of evicting his wife. Wilkinson was of course 'spok'n to' and 'advice given' which first appeared to calm him down but suddenly found himself confronted by Wilkinson waving a poker at him and threatening 'to do' for him.

Once again he was pacified but again returned to his door snarling abusive and obscene language at the officer. Enough is enough, and Wilkinson found himself summoned to appear before Gateshead Magistrates on Friday 25th January, where he was fined 2/6d with 6/- costs, a considerable sum for the day.

The fate of PC Graham was now sealed. Both men made their own way back to the village some three miles distant from the court PC Graham arriving at 'The Princess Alice Inn' on the outskirts of the village at about 3.20pm the officer made his way home to Springfield Terrace where he lived with his wife and four children. Later on that day Wilkinson would see him out and decide to attack him.

Gatesheadpolice.org

As spectators gathered, Wilkinson crept behind the unaware policeman. Then, grabbing the policeman by the arm from behind, the Flying Butcher spun him around and plunged the knife into the right side of his chest. As PC Graham staggered across the road and fell onto the grass, Wilkinson grabbed the dying officer's truncheon and rained blows at his head.

The Flying Butcher then stormed off towards Eighton Banks, threatening to kill another policeman. As PC Graham's corpse was laid out back in his nearby home, and as news of the killing spread, search parties were sent out to capture Wilkinson, who apparently called into three pubs bragging about his actions. He was finally captured at the Railway Tavern in South Hylton with the knife concealed on him.

On 26 February 1889, Wilkinson was found guilty of murder at Durham Assizes, where he interrupted the sentencing judge with a cry of: 'Oh let's have it! It's no use bothering ...'

Incredibly he was able to escape being hanged after being reprieved on the grounds of insanity.

GEORDIE PIRATE

Edward Robinson is a name one might not associate with a pirate, however that is the name of a Newcastle man who sailed under one of history's most infamous pirates, Black Beard. Edward was said to have been born in a pub on the Newcastle Quayside named the Beehive, now named Red House, to a mother who was a prostitute. Legend has it that after an altercation with another man at the nearby pub the White Hart Inn, Edward slit his throat and threw the body into the Tyne before fleeing the country.

Though little is known about parts of his life, it is believed Edward made his way to America and is listed as being a crew member of Stede Bonnet, also known as the Gentleman Pirate. Sailing under a black flag on board his ship the *Revenge*, witnesses say Edward bore arms 'Freely and voluntarily'. Following the taking of the ship *Adventure* he is listed as the ship's gunner, being responsible for the ten guns on board the *Revenge* used for persuading other ships to submit to their will. The *Revenge* may have been owned by Stede Bonnet but it was part of a fleet of pirate ships, the largest of which was referred to as *The Great Devil,* whose captain was Edward Thatch, also known as Black Beard.

Black Beard was said to have taken over the *Revenge* following Stede's wounding during a clash with a Spanish man-of-war. It was here his true reign of terror began, and after conquering the *Adventure* he sailed north, looting and pillaging much on his way. They eventually made their way to Charleston in South Carolina, where a blockade was set up in the town's harbour with a number of ships being seized. The pirates demanded a chest of medicine otherwise they would execute all their prisoners and it is reported one of those who wished to deliver these demands was Edward Robinson. He was not selected to go ashore, however, the crew received their ransom after five days and Black Beard made off with his reward and the loot taken from the ships.

The fleet continued heading north and it is said Black Beard deliberately marooned some of the men following a wreck, in the hope of breaking up his large pirate crew to secure more of the treasure for himself and close companions. Edward was one of the seventeen stranded men left on a sandbank without food, water or shade to await a long, painful death. The men were rescued by Stede Bonnet, who offered them a chance to re-join the crew of the *Revenge*, now fully under his control. Although Bonnet was returning from receiving a pardon when he saw the marooned men, he continued living the pirate life by raiding passing ships and, in August 1718, he encountered the sloop *Francis*. The taking of this ship seemed to be the final straw and a bounty was placed on Stede and his crew by Governor Robert Johnson, who was determined to end the reign of terror.

The crimes of these men eventually caught up with them and after a long drawn-out battle with casualties on both sides the pirate crew were forced to surrender. Stede, Robinson and the crew were brought to Charleston and those who had previous encounters with them were brought to testify against them. The men were given no legal counsel but allowed to make cases for themselves, with many testifying they were forced to live this life out of desperation. All men were found guilty, and on 8 November 1718 Edward and twenty-eight others were hanged before a baying crowd. The long drop method of hanging had not been invented at this point, so many would have watched as Robinson struggled at the end of a rope for more than ten minutes waiting to die of strangulation.

This event remains one of the largest mass hangings in history and although Stede Bonnet did initially escape he was recaptured and suffered the same fate as his men two days later. Black Beard outlived them by only a few weeks and was killed in a battle with the pirate hunter Robert Maynard of HMS *Pearl* in North Carolina. He was decapitated and his head was hung from the bowsprit of Maynard's ship. The death of the Newcastle pirate Edward Robinson some 4,000 miles away from his home town was to mark the beginning of the end of the golden age of piracy. For further reading on this, I recommend the book *Sins Dyed In Blood: The Lost Pirate of Blackbeard's Golden Age* by author Paul Brown.

CATS AS FOOD

Ann Little was 54 years old in 1885 when she was charged with theft. While in police custody other charges were brought against her and her house was searched, leading the police to a disturbing discovery.

The remains of multiple bodies of cats were found buried in the garden and around the property, which alone would be enough to alarm anyone. However, what made the situation worse was that large numbers of people had been buying 'Scotch hares' from the woman. Ann had even reassured curious buyers about the difference in taste from regular hare soup, saying it was due to their nationality.

More than fifty people turned up at the police station to look for their pets and as many as fifteen persons were seen digging in her garden. Ann was sentenced to three months' imprisonment and when charged for the offence had this to say: 'I have sold several, and we have eaten several ourselves; they are very like a rabbit when cooked.'

DEADLY DANCE MOVES

In November 1878 an argument took place between two men over who was the better dancer, a row that would prove to be fatal. John Hart, a 21-year-old miner, had spent the day out shopping with his sister when the two became separated and, rather than go home, he decided to call in at his uncle's house in Elswick Street. The two decided to go out for a walk and while out called into a local beer house named The Queens Arms on Westgate Road. There John met a man with whom he was previously acquainted named Thomas Richardson.

John knew Thomas somewhat as the two had previously worked together at the colliery as miners. Thomas is reported to have been a few years older than John but it is said the two greeted each other and had a drink together. At some point during the conversation the topic of dancing came up and a dispute arose between the two men as to who was the best. The conversation escalated very quickly as Thomas would not back down about his dancing prowess and his temper rose to a point that the barman had to eject him from the building. He was reported to have come back into the bar and was ejected once more, only this time it seemed to have resolved the matter. However, half an hour later John left the bar with his uncle only to find Thomas waiting outside, intent on resuming the dancing dispute. John, however, was not interested and attempted to resolve the quarrel, even going so far as to invite Thomas to another nearby place named the Goat Inn for a drink.

The two became separated by a short distance and John was reported to have pretended to run at Thomas a few times but he would always run away. Thomas then shouted to John to come down the street and that he would 'fettle him', and although cautioned by his friends, John went close to him in the hope of resolving the situation. When John got near he attempted to shake his hand, hoping to put an end to the situation, to which Thomas accepted by grabbing his hand and stabbing him three times in the torso. John fell to the ground and Thomas immediately fled the scene as the wounded man was taken to his uncle's nearby. John's wounds proved fatal and although his killer initially escaped he was caught in disguise the next day.

At first Thomas is reported to have said, 'I know nowt about it,' but the blood-marked knife was soon recovered. He was then imprisoned and charged with wilful murder, being found guilty and sentenced to death. Whilst condemned in Newcastle Gaol he no doubt thought a great deal about how he would dance no more, that is until the governor received a letter from the Home Secretary ordering the cancellation of his execution. His lucky escape from death was thanks to a petition signed by a number of people, including the Mayor of Newcastle, stating that a prison sentence would better suit his crime. Thomas Richardson escaped the gallows for his dancing-related crimes but no doubt the family of John Hart would have felt justice was not served.

Did you know that some of the first ships built to send convicted criminals from Britain to Australia were made in Sunderland?

The *Borrowdale* – Built at Hylton in 1785, was one of the First Fleet, a convoy of eleven ships that transported the first convicts and settlers to Australia.

The *William Hammond* – Built in 1853 in Sunderland for Thomas and Co.

The HMS *Investigator* – Built by Henry Rudd in Monkwearmouth in 1795, it was the first ship used to circumnavigate Australia.

The *Dunbar* – At its launch it was the largest timber ship built in Sunderland. It met an unfortunate fate when it ran aground near Sydney Harbour and all its passengers but one perished, a total of 121 people drowning.

Convict transportation to Australia ended in January 1868. Approximately 164,000 convicts were transported to the Australian colonies between 1788 and 1868 on board 806 ships.

CHARLES SMITH AND THE HUMAN SKIN BOOK

Locked away in the depths of Newcastle Library lies an old book that at a glance may warrant little attention. It details the execution of Newcastle resident Charles Smith, who was hanged for murder in 1817. The well-preserved relic mostly consists of a collection of articles related to the execution, with the exception of one very macabre page that stands out. It is of leather-like quality and if reports are to be believed it is the skin of Charles Smith himself.

One dark night on 4 December 1816, a break-in took place at a pottery in Ouseburn, a once-bustling industrial area on the outskirts of Newcastle city centre. Charles Stewart, the resident caretaker, was asleep within the premises, tasked with protecting the property. That night he was beaten severely by two intruders to the point of almost passing away there and then. His legs were bound together and his head covered, ultimately being left for dead after the vicious attack. With the keeper removed from the equation, the pottery was pillaged and the intruders escaped. Stewart, however, did not succumb to his injuries overnight and had recovered by the morning, able to describe the vicious attack and, perhaps most importantly, accuse a man whose voice he recognised as being one of the criminals. It was that of Irishman Charles Smith. Stewart died of his injuries that same month but swore his claims were correct until his moment of death.

Smith was tried and protested his innocence all the way until the rope was put around his neck and he was hanged. His last words, as reported by the *Carlisle Patriot* on 13 December 1817, were said to be:

As I am going to meet my God, I do declare that I never shed the blood of Charles Stewart nor that of any human creature, nor had I ever such intention, nor did ever such an idea enter my mind, as I always had the greatest abhorrence of murder ... I deny the whole ... but I forgive all from my heart, and hope God will forgive them.

WINTER OF TERROR

The winters of the early 1800s were dark and cold ones with few residents being brave enough to venture from the comfort of their homes on cold evenings. Oil lamps illuminated the narrow alleyways and streets, accompanied by figures who would disappear when someone tried to grab their attention as if they were shadows. Bodies began disappearing from the Holy Trinity churchyard at an alarming rate and fear soon gripped the people of Sunderland.

The names Burke and Hare will be familiar to some but, if the book *Alice in Sunderland* is to be believed, few will know of their venture to Sunderland. While there, they are said to have pillaged the resting place of its dead in 1820. The infamous duo, who were dubbed resurrectionists, would transport and sell the bodies of the deceased to the equally notorious Dr Robert Knox in Edinburgh for dissection at his anatomy lectures, for which they were paid handsomely. In Sunderland, it is reported that Hare would stand at the Old Market entrance in Coronation Street bellowing, 'Chelsea buns. Pies all hot, mutton pies.' Nearby, his partner Burke did the diabolical deed, listening for the cries to cease so as to know when he was in danger of being caught.

Another grizzly tale of body snatching in Sunderland's east end is the legend of Half-Hanged Jack. Jack was said to be a local body snatcher who put the corpses of women in a sack, to which he tied a rope around its centre in an attempt to lift the bodies over the churchyard wall. During the grim process Jack was said to have become caught in the rope and as the sack slipped through, the rope tightened around his neck and he hung from the rope until he was found by a watchman half alive and half dead. His injuries would prove fatal, as he died shortly after but his spirit is said to have continued to haunt the graveyard.

Grave robbing became so bad that security was tightened in 1824 to a point where it was reported a sparrow could not steal a worm from the churchyard without being caught. By this point Burke and Hare were said to have been long gone, however their crimes did not go unpunished as in their desperation, rather than digging up bodies, they began murdering people. Suspicions grew, and while it is said there was little evidence linking the men to these crimes, Hare was offered immunity to turn against his fiendish friend. He obliged and confessed to his involvement in the sixteen murders the pair had committed as well as other crimes. Burke was hanged shortly afterwards, his corpse dissected and his skeleton donated to the Anatomical Museum of the Edinburgh Medical School, where it is believed to be today. Hare seems to have been followed by his crimes, with angry mobs forming when they learned who he was. Nothing is known of his final days as he disappeared but it is rumoured he died a pauper in London.

THE GRIM END OF SIR WILLIAM WALLACE

Born around 1270, very little is known about the early years of Sir William Wallace's life other than unconfirmed reports that his family were landowners. In 1296, Edward I decided to take advantage of the succession crisis in Scotland following the death of the Scottish King Alexander III and his subsequent heir some years earlier.

Numerous families laid claim to the throne and amidst the chaos King Edward I of England became involved, imposing an English administration across Scotland. It was not long before civil unrest broke out, thus providing the backdrop for Wallace's rise to fame. While some sources suggest he had rebelled against the English before by killing soldiers, it was not until he murdered the English High Sheriff William de Heselrig of Lanark in May 1297 that his name became known.

What began as civil unrest then erupted into a full-blown rebellion, with men flocking from across Scotland to fight alongside William. He began driving the English out of Perthshire and Fife before his infamous defeat of a much larger English force at the Battle of Stirling Bridge in September 1297. This and other military successes led to the significant weakening of Edward I's control on Scotland and William then marched south.

Laying siege to parts of Northumberland and causing many in the area to flee to Newcastle, the Scottish freedom fighter wreaked havoc

on the North East. It is also said he was prepared to march on Durham, however bad weather and rumours of a fortified force awaiting made him change his mind. The English then rallied around Edward I and led an army up north, determined to put a stop to the chaos.

In 1298 both armies clashed near Falkirk and the Scottish rebels suffered a brutal defeat, losing many men. Wallace escaped with his life but his reputation was damaged and he soon stepped down as Guardian of Scotland in favour of Robert the Bruce. While in France searching for support for Scottish independence, Robert the Bruce and John Comyn came to terms with the English in a deal that excluded Wallace.

William was captured in 1305 and taken to the Tower of London to be executed. Charged with treason among other crimes, he is alleged to have stated, 'I could not be a traitor to Edward, for I was never his subject.' He was dragged naked through the city before being hung, drawn and quartered. His head was placed on a spike on London Bridge, while the four corners of his mutilated body were sent to Berwick, Perth, Stirling and Newcastle. It is reported to have been one of the right-side sections of body that was sent to the North East and is thought to have been displayed on the old Tyne Bridge.

JACK THE RIPPER CONNECTION

Jack the Ripper is a name that conjures up images of horrific crimes perpetrated during the Victorian era in England by a killer whose identity is still debated today. Perhaps England's most infamous serial killer, Jack the Ripper continues to capture the imagination of those who read about him but few know about his possible connection to Gateshead.

On 23 September 1888 in the small mining village of Birtley the shocking discovery of the mutilated body of a woman named Jane Beadmore made many question whether the notorious killer had made his way to the area. The day before her body was discovered, Jane had left her home to travel to Newcastle in hopes of seeing a doctor as she reportedly felt unwell. Following her return home, Jane left her parents' house to visit some friends who lived only a short distance away. She stayed here until the early evening and when she left visited Mount Moor public house, drinking only a bottle of lemonade, before visiting a tobacco shop to purchase some sweets. The last sighting of Jane was by a man who saw her heading in the opposite direction to her home after 8.30 p.m.

The following morning her body was discovered by a local mechanic. She had been dead for a number of hours and the local police constable was immediately informed. There appeared to be no sign of a struggle, although her hands were covering her face in a bid to protect herself. No bloodstains were found near her body but her clothes were reportedly saturated with blood and robbery was ruled out as a motive due to what little money she had being found still in her pocket. The examination of her body revealed horrific wounds stretching from her cheek to neck on one side and a similar wound on the other side as well. A large gash in her abdomen had opened her body, with the wounds appearing to have been inflicted with a sharp knife.

The shocking nature of the attack made many struggle to believe a local man could have been so brutal and people began to point the finger at Jack the Ripper. Dr Phillips, who conducted the post-mortem examination on Annie Chapman, the last victim of the Whitechapel murders, was brought to Gateshead to ascertain if the injuries were similar to that of the Whitechapel victim. Scotland Yard detectives came to investigate and papers began publishing headlines such as 'Revolting tragedy near Gateshead. Has the East End killer gone north?'

The funeral was said to have attracted huge crowds, with many travelling great distances to attend. One theory that immediately stuck is that it was not Jack the Ripper, but rather Jane's former lover whose advances she spurned due to her interest in a new man. William Waddell had not been seen since the discovery of the cruel crime and he remained at large until 8 October, when he was found looking 'wild and jaded'. Waddell was immediately brought to police, where he was put in a cell and interrogated about the events. He initially denied knowing Jane but later allegedly confessed to the crime. His transportation to inner Gateshead by train drew thousands of curious onlookers all hoping to catch a glimpse of the accused man. His barrister, Mr Skidmore, was said to have put up a spirited defence of his client but in the end Waddell was sentenced to death.

On 18 December, William Waddell was hanged. The connection to the Jack the Ripper murders was dismissed but there are still some who doubt the conviction. There are numerous cases that have been linked to the infamous killer, as well as many theories about his identity. It seems unlikely this tragic local event was connected to the Ripper but the mere suggestion certainly caused a stir in the county.

WALKING THE PLANK

The phrase 'walking the plank' refers to a method of execution used by pirates, mutineers and rogue seafarers. For this method a plank would be placed leading over the ship into the sea and the unfortunate victim would often be tied up and forced to walk along into the crashing waves below.

In 1885 one newspaper report references two stowaways from Sunderland who were caught after sneaking on board the ship *Regina* destined for New Orleans with a cargo of coal. This would not have been uncommon as young men all over the country would often sneak aboard ships hoping to land somewhere with more opportunities. When the ship stopped at Dover the young men were put aboard a boat and sent ashore, which cost the captain 25*s*. Once the boat arrived the stowaways were said to be very frightened as the captain had threatened to make them walk the plank, a threat the boys took seriously.

In another tale in July 1870, a man in North Shields was brought before the courts, described as being a vagabond. The man accosted people in the street, brandishing a wooden sign that read:

'Twenty-six years ago, I was a sailor on board the ship *Marianne*, of Liverpool. In the Archipelago we were boarded by Greek pirates, when the captain was made to walk the plank. Three of the crew got their ears cut off, three their hands and three their tongues cut out, of which last three I am one – John Brown.'

The cunning police officers coaxed the man into speaking, proving his story to be fraudulent and resulting in him being committed for a month.

Instances of people being made to walk the plank throughout history are few and far between. This brutal form of punishment seems to have only been reserved for use by outlaws and criminals, with a small number of documented cases having evidence. Although rarely reported, the terrifying images walking the plank conjures up have secured its place within sea-related lore and fiction alike.

MARY ANN COTTON

Largely credited with being Britain's first female serial killer and certainly the North East's most notorious, it is believed Mary Ann Cotton may have murdered up to as many as twenty-one people. To poison her victims she chiefly used arsenic, which was tasteless and caused gastric pain and a rapid decline in health.

It is likely that she murdered three out of four of her husbands to collect on their insurance policies and many others, including eleven of her thirteen children. At a time when there was little food and few job opportunities, bad record keeping and constant movement of people, it would not have been uncommon for her crimes to go unnoticed for longer.

She was arrested in January 1873 and charged over the death of Charles Edward Cotton. She was sentenced to death and was to be hanged at Durham Gaol two months later. Her execution, however, did not go as planned and she did not die from her neck breaking. Instead she died from strangulation as the rope had been rigged too short, some say deliberately.

THE MERRY WIDOW OF WINDY NOOK

In a more recent case of a black widow, Mary Elizabeth Wilson was a British serial killer born in County Durham in 1893. Mary moved to a suburb in Windy Nook in Gateshead with her first husband, John Knowles, in around 1914 and she lived there for more than forty years.

Her lover, John Russell, moved in with the couple as a lodger then shortly after, in 1955, her husband passed away. Mary waited five months before marrying Russell, who died a year or so later, with both deaths recorded as natural causes. Mary inherited money from both of her husbands and went on to marry a third man in 1957. Oliver Lennord, Mary's third husband, died twelve days into his new marriage, leaving her more money. She soon married again, this time to a man named Ernest Wilson who had a larger estate and a life insurance policy. He too died within a year and this time Mary reportedly did not bother to attend the funeral.

By this point gossip had begun to spread around the area about the rate at which Mary seemed to be going through husbands. People often remarked at her cheerful attitude during the times of mourning. Mary even joked at her latest wedding reception that left-over sandwiches could be kept for the funeral. Another story tells how she tried asking for a trade discount from the funeral director for providing him with so much business. It is said these instances of morbid humour are what brought her to the attention of the police.

The bodies of her last two husbands were exhumed and were found to contain high levels of phosphorous, indicating they had been poisoned. Mary was found guilty of the two murders and sentenced to death in Durham in 1958. A subsequent investigation also revealed the same pattern when her first two husbands were exhumed, proving she had murdered all four of them. Her advanced age allowed her a reprieve and she was instead sentenced to life imprisonment. Mary Wilson died while incarcerated in Holloway in 1963.

THE LEGEND OF HALF HUNG MACDONALD

On the evening of 23 May 1752, Ewan MacDonald, a member of the 42nd Highlanders, was drinking in Newcastle's Bigg Market. A fight broke out in the pub and the chaos soon spilled outside, where MacDonald then stabbed a man named Robert Park in the neck. Robert died almost immediately but MacDonald wasn't finished there and returned inside the pub, where he is said to have continued brawling and broke another man's arm.

MacDonald was soon arrested and found guilty of wilful murder, being sentenced to hang on the town moor. Ewan, who was only 19 years old at the time, was executed on 28 September and it is said he showed great remorse for his actions while in confinement. While on the gallows he made one final futile show of defiance by throwing the executioner off his ladder.

His body was taken to the surgeons' hall ready for dissection, but the surgeons were called to deal with something urgent in the infirmary. Upon their return they found the young man alive and sitting up. The story goes that he begged for mercy, only to have his life ended by a wooden mallet and he was dissected as planned.

DANGEROUS DIVING

Born on the Isle of Wight in 1835, Stephen Jeffrey was a man who enjoyed local fame for a brief period in the 1800s. In reports he states that he was at the Crimean War and the Indian Mutiny before moving to Sunderland, where he describes himself as a professional diver.

The first feat he performed that caught everyone's attention was to dive from the Wearmouth Bridge into the River Wear in 1865. Despite being refused permission for his jump, handbills were circulated so as to draw an audience to witness his dangerous stunt. His routine was to throw an orange over the side of the bridge, then put his hat on and jump off. Donations would then be taken afterwards. Jeffrey miraculously survived this jump and set his sights on the next one.

When word began to spread of Jeffrey saying he would next jump from the High Level Bridge in Newcastle into the Tyne River, the authorities began to worry. This bridge was considerably higher and arguably in a more dangerous position, but Jeffrey was not concerned. In May the same year crowds gathered to watch the diver perform his deadly feat but as time went on many grew concerned he would not appear. From far away the audience could see a figure get out of a taxi and hurl himself off the bridge, it soon transpired though that it was a straw dummy dressed in a sailor's costume thrown over by a joker. Despite efforts to save the man made of straw, he was not alive when boats finally reached him. Next up was a man who also wanted to entertain the crowd and decided to wade into the Tyne, but he was soon arrested and charged with being drunk and disorderly.

It was not long before confirmation of the date of Jeffrey's next attempt to jump the bridge was set. Again a massive crowd gathered, bringing traffic to a standstill and drawing a large police presence. Despite denying to police that he intended to jump, he arrived in a cab from Gateshead before taking his place on the bridge and throwing his orange over first. The police were prepared this time and, although he struggled with them, he was arrested and brought into custody, with a police escort struggling to contain the riotous scenes that erupted. Stones were hurled at the officers and masses of people surged through the city, upset at not getting the chance to witness the bizarre spectacle.

Jeffrey was accused of being drunk at the time and was put on trial. Unable to pay a fine, he was sentenced to a week in jail before convincing the magistrate he would not attempt the feat again if he was let go. He returned to Sunderland and in June he joined with the crew of HMS *Active* to take part in a display of rocket apparatus used to save lives. I could find little more information on him after this but it seems he applied to the Sunderland courts for permission to jump from the bridge into the river again in 1880. This seems to have been denied and with that Stephen Jeffrey disappeared from the spotlight.

5

TRAGEDY

The phrase 'it's grim up north' is one that is often uttered by those who may not have heard or seen the beauty referred to in some of the other chapters of this book, but nonetheless it is one that may sadly be true in the following stories. From diseases to accidents, tragedy has been borne in many different ways up here, and although I would not wish it on anyone I would like to think we are all the stronger for it.

AN AERONAUT'S ACCIDENT

In August 1859, William Hall made an ascent from Northumberland Cricket Ground in Newcastle in a balloon. Known as aeronauts, those who bravely travelled to the sky in balloons often drew a large crowd eager to see man beat gravity.

On this day thousands are said to have gathered to watch Hall, with many climbing onto roofs to catch a glimpse. Beginning at approximately 6 p.m., the initial stages of his performance went well with him safely reaching an impressive height, to the amazement of those watching. He then climbed onto ropes dangling beneath the balloon and began performing trapeze-like poses while hanging above the earth. The performance ended with the balloon travelling off into the distance, at which point Hall intended to bring the balloon down in the village of Boldon.

It seems the wind had other plans, however, as Hall was prevented from making his ideal landing. When the grappling hook used to bring the balloon down failed he was thrown about the basket, becoming entangled in the netting. Numerous attempts to reach safety failed and Hall ended up falling from a height of over 100ft head first to the ground below. He was immediately rushed to the house of local man, Hugh Lee Pattison, where a doctor from Newcastle who happened to be nearby attended to him.

One particularly sad part of this story is that Hall was not alone on his flight in the balloon. The aeronaut had got into the habit of taking his little dog into the sky with him as he believed it brought him luck. While Hall had escaped the balloon, his dog did not and was instead flying about in the sky by itself. William Hall's injuries proved fatal within a week and he died at the age of 39 in Newcastle Infirmary. What became of his dog is a mystery but some believed that due to the direction of the wind it landed in the sea.

THE PLAGUE

While the plague had visited the region before, it particularly devastated the North East in 1636. It is believed to have originated in North Shields, possibly brought in by one of the many rats passing through the busy port. The sickness spread rapidly through the county, with high death tolls being recorded in many cities.

Some of the symptoms included bleeding from the mouth or nose, gangrenous skin and large boils that could grow to the size of apples. Many victims would be boarded up in their homes with crosses painted on the doors to warn of the contagion. It is reported that between May and December of that year more than 5,631 out of an approximate population of 12,000 died in Newcastle alone.

Many of the corpses of those who had contracted the plague in Newcastle were carted off to be dumped into pits at parish churches like St Nicholas Church in the town centre.

PARACHUTISTS

Knowledge relating to air resistance being capable of slowing down items falling from a height has existed for thousands of years. However, it was not until the 1700s that Frenchman Louis-Sébastien Lenormand plucked up the courage to throw himself from the tower of the Montpellier observatory using an early prototype, and developments in the field of parachuting began to happen. While I have already covered famous balloonists who visited Tyne and Wear, this section will cover interesting female parachutists.

In the 1800s parachutists became a common spectacle in the North East due to advances in this field of technology. One of the most well-known lady parachutists was Alma Beaumont, an American, believed to have been born in Nebraska. In 1889 she put on a number of shows, including one in North Shields in August that drew thousands of spectators. Getting into position in her balloon, the lines were cut and Alma sailed off into the air until all that could be seen was a small dot. Anxiety gripped the audience as she fell with great speed towards the earth, only for onlookers to be relieved when the parachute opened successfully and she landed in a field near Spittal Dene, surprising a number of cows. After safely returning from her trip up to 15,000ft, the crowd greeted Alma with praise and she had won the hearts of all who witnessed the feat.

Her descent was not always as successful, unfortunately, as was the case with one incident that occurred in October the same year. Starting in Jarrow this time, Alma ventured skyward once more, prepared to make the swift return. The parachute deployed successfully but perhaps due to wind she was swept in the direction of the Tyne. Landing in the river near Howdon Dock, she was promptly rescued by a small boat and was described as being little worse for wear.

As the popularity of parachutists rose, so did the number of accidents to those involved. In 1896 a 14-year-old female parachutist, billed as Mademoiselle Albertina, perished on her first run from Cardiff, with her body being found in the Bristol Channel. Another fatal accident in 1902 saw first-time lady parachutist Edith Brooks fall to her death after ascending from Sheffield Football Ground, much to the horror of her sister, also a lady parachutist.

Due to the rising number of accidents, a public outcry for women to be banned from being parachutists arose. The Wright Brothers' invention of the aeroplane in 1903 would also see the steady decline of balloonists and parachutists alike. At a time when women did not have the right to vote there is no doubt that Alma and the other lady parachutists showed more courage than most men.

CHOLERA PANDEMIC

What is generally considered the first cholera pandemic occurred in Bengal in 1816 and spread across India and much of Asia. In 1831 the second cholera pandemic began and this time it was believed to have started in Russia. It reached Sunderland first in the United Kingdom, spreading through the port.

Despite a quarantine of ships from the Baltic states, one docked in Sunderland and brought cholera with it. From here the disease spread up and down the country, claiming more than 52,000 lives. This came at a time when germs were not properly understood and one popular theory on how the disease spread was miasma theory. Now obsolete, this theory supposed that noxious air was responsible for the spread of the disease and that it originated from rotting organic matter.

The disease hit the North East hard, with the death toll in Sunderland alone reaching more than 200. Cemeteries were overcrowded and ships leaving the city were quarantined. The disease spread quickest among the working classes and reports of it spreading across Tyne and Wear due to relatives visiting each other were common.

On 9 January 1832, the Board of Health declared that Sunderland was free of cholera and by the end of that year the epidemic was coming to end. Cholera did resurface in Britain in 1848, claiming almost twice as many lives as it did during the first epidemic in certain parts of the country.

THE GREAT FLOOD

On 17 November 1771, continuous heavy rainfall led to a great flood, causing massive destruction to many parts of the North East. The water raged through the city, uprooting coffins from cemeteries and leaving many houses and shops underwater. A build-up of water also led to the destruction of large portions of the old Tyne Bridge.

The book *An Account of the Great Flood in the Rivers Tyne, Tees, Wear and Eden* recorded some of the events that took place. One story tells of a Mr Fiddas who lived on the north side of the bridge who managed to escape with his wife and maidservant. However, having made it to safety, the maidservant convinced Mr Fiddas to return with her to save some of her possessions. The arch of the bridge collapsed beneath them and Mrs Fiddas watched her husband and servant get swept away.

While many people lost their lives, the book does recount stories of incredible luck and bravery. A cradle was found floating near Shields with a baby still inside alive. Another tale recounts how a Mr Patton had his house and all his belongings swept away, only for his house to be found later with his cat and dog surviving inside. Peter Weatherly, a shoemaker who also lived on the bridge, ended up stranded when both sides collapsed around him. The shocked onlookers dared not rescue them as it was still far too dangerous, but after some hours a bricklayer from Gateshead climbed across the rooftops to get the family to safety.

CHANGING THE RULES OF THE GAME

Jimmy Thorpe was an English footballer born in Jarrow in 1913. He was signed at 17 to Sunderland, where he was a goalkeeper and played in 139 games. It was during a game at Roker Park on 1 February 1936, where Sunderland were playing Chelsea, that a tragic accident would prove fatal for Jimmy.

Jimmy went to grab the ball after a back pass when he was kicked in the head and chest. He continued to take part in the match despite his injuries but was taken to hospital once the match was over. Jimmy slipped into a diabetic coma due to the injuries he received and passed away on 5 February aged 22.

After Jimmy's death the rules were changed to stop players kicking the ball out of the goalkeeper's hands. Sunderland went on to win the championship that year and a medal was presented to his widow.

TRAGEDY ON THE TYNE

On the evening of Monday, 6 May 1867, a horrific accident occurred at Newcastle quayside in front of hundreds of shocked spectators. An audience of thousands had been out to watch a boat race and had begun to make their way home. The landing stage of the Tyne General Ferry Company was moored approximately 80ft from the public quay and was connected by a wooden bridge. At 7 p.m. it was estimated that more than a hundred people stood on the gangway eagerly awaiting their chance to secure a spot on the ferry, with many more stood near the quay.

Without warning, a thunderous crack was heard and the bridge gave way, plunging the mass of jostling people into the river below. Scenes of indescribable confusion were reported to have ensued as people scrambled to cling on to the bridge against the strong current. The waters of the Tyne were said to be almost hidden under the sea of terrified faces looking up to those who might be able to help. The heroic actions of those nearby undoubtedly saved many lives as people dived into boats and keels, stretching out arms and poles to rescue as many people as possible.

One story tells how one young couple were stood with their arms round one another's waists when the bridge collapsed, both sinking under the water together and getting carried by the current. Neither lost their grip of the other and they were lucky enough to drift close enough to a boat, where the young woman grabbed an outstretched leg and pulled them to safety. Another tells how a sailor from Shields named David Tarrs was on the gangway when it went down, but instead of escaping himself he saved the lives of five other men before becoming so ill that he too needed assistance.

Unfortunately, not all were as lucky that day, as is the case with a Mr Foster of the River Police, who was near at the time. It is reported he grabbed onto a post as he climbed down to better pull people up when he managed to grab onto a drowning man. The man was seen as their best chance to escape and seized upon in such a way that people became entangled. Foster, feeling his strength dissipate, was forced to let go or be pulled into the river himself. He believed the tangled group of people to be ten strong and that they had sunk to the river bed after he let go as he did not see them again.

Exact figures for how many lives were lost that day on the Newcastle Quayside are unknown but some estimates place the number as high as 200. This tragic chapter in North East history made newspapers all over the world but is now largely forgotten.

THE TYNE BRIDGE

Construction of the Tyne Bridge as we know it began in 1925, and it was officially opened three years later by King George V and Queen Mary. The total cost of construction was £1.2 million. It is believed that one of the first bridges across the Tyne was built by the Romans near to where the current Tyne Bridge stands, and was named Pons Aelius.

One unfortunate loss of life was recorded during construction, on 19 February 1928. While working 175ft atop the bridge, Nathaniel Collins, a scaffolder from South Shields, slipped and fell from the great height. Another man, John James Carr, rowed to the spot where Nathaniel had entered the water and dived in, risking his own life to save him. However, due to a strong tide both men were washed a quarter of a mile down the river before finally being rescued by another boat. Nathaniel was rushed to Newcastle Infirmary but sadly died of his injuries.

On another note, on 28 June 2012 a large lightning bolt struck the bridge, lighting up the sky. The bolt was part of a supercell thunderstorm and came with a month's worth of rainfall in two hours, causing flash flooding in many parts of Tyneside.

THE FLYING DONKEY

During the seventeenth century flying men were very popular. They would climb heights and throw themselves off, often with a rope attached like a bungie, but these displays frequently resulted in their death.

One such flying man came to Newcastle Castle in 1733 and planned to jump off the castle keep with wings attached, drawing a huge crowd of spectators. Upon reaching his jumping point and looking at the 100ft drop below, he decided he would first put the wings on a donkey for a test flight.

The donkey was forced off the drop and landed on the horrified crowd, injuring many and resulting in the death of a young girl.

While the donkey survived, little is known about what happened to the flying man afterwards.

A TRAGIC RESCUE ATTEMPT

On 9 August 1886, a 9-year-old boy named John Lennon was out playing with two of his friends near Messrs Allhusen's Chemical Works, South Shore, Gateshead. John fell 15ft down a ventilation shaft of a drain and was unable to get out.

A 25-year-old man of the surname Swinburn was first to come to the child's rescue. After climbing down, he managed to grab hold of the boy but while climbing back out was overpowered by the sewer gas and fell back to the bottom of the shaft, unable to get out. Another man by the name of Thomas Quinn then descended into the shaft in the hope of being able to rescue the trapped pair, but after only a few steps he too was overpowered by the noxious vapours and fell to the bottom.

At this point another man, named Edward Scullion, went and collected a protective mask and rope and lowered himself into the shaft. Edward attached the rope to the man, the lad and the boy, elevating them to ground level. The doctor was sent for but it was already too late for Lennon and Quinn, who were pronounced dead. Swinburn survived until 11 p.m. the following evening before also passing away. Edward Scullion was awarded the Albert Medal for his actions.

A memorial to this unfortunate chapter in local history was erected in Durham Road in Gateshead. It stood for a number of years but was removed in 1969.

MADAME FRANCK'S FLYING ACCIDENT

Born in 1866, Rosalind Mathilde Franck was one of the earliest female French aviators. She had first learned to fly at the Farman brothers' manufacturing plant near Paris in 1910 and quickly gained attention when she piloted a successful non-stop 14-mile flight at Mourmelon.

The next goal she had set her sights on was to cross the Channel, however this was postponed due to weather.

In late July 1910 she arrived in the North East and met the manager of the Sunderland Empire to participate in flight demonstrations at the Boldon Races. On 30 July she accomplished a flight of a mile and a half, which is believed to be the first significant distance covered by a woman in the United Kingdom. On the following Monday she attempted the feat again, however this time it ended in disaster.

Billed as the 'Parisian Airwoman', her performance at Boldon Racecourse is reported to have drawn a crowd of more than 7,000 people. Her display got off to a good start as she soared above the audience in her Farman biplane but some were concerned by how close to the ground she was flying. After taking a longer detour towards the direction of the sea she returned, narrowly missing a row of houses. However, as she was coming down she clipped a flagstaff, with the plane bringing both crashing down.

Thomas Wood, aged 15, was killed in the crash. Reports state he was either hit by the propeller or engine, which almost cut him in half and killed him almost instantly. Numerous other spectators were hurt, but Madame Franck miraculously survived. She was first taken into one of the nearby cottages and attended to by a doctor before being taken to Sunderland Infirmary. Her injuries included a fracture in two places to her left leg and a bad cut on her throat.

While this unfortunate piece of aviation history is seldom mentioned locally any more, the impact it had on Madame Franck was lasting. The events in Boldon put an end to her flying career and she never obtained her licence.

THE AMBOYNA MASSACRE

The Amboyna Massacre, which took place in 1623 on the Indonesian island of Ambon, is a piece of English history that is now largely forgotten. Fierce competition between the English East India Company and the Dutch East India Company created a bitter rivalry that would see the execution of twenty men on a small island far from home.

The island of Ambon at this time was inhabited by both English and Dutch forces co-operatively sharing the land. Distrust by both sides saw tensions rise in the weeks prior to blood being spilled until it reached a critical point. Japanese mercenaries, also known as Ronin, in the employment of the Dutch company are said to have been caught spying on the defences of their fort. When one of the Ronin was caught and tortured he was forced to turn on the other Japanese on the island, who in turn blamed the English.

The Englishmen were rounded up and arrested before being interrogated on the matter. One method used on the unfortunate men was to have a burning hot poker forced under the armpit as well as the palms of their hands, in the hope they would reveal information. The next method employed is sometimes referred to as the water cure and it involved forcing as much water down the men's throats as possible without killing them, in a similar manner to modern-day waterboarding. With no other choice the men turned on each other, admitting guilt to get a reprieve from the horrors they endured. As a result of their confessions the men were sentenced to death but not before the island natives were gathered and the prisoners paraded before them.

One of the Englishmen awaiting his sentence to be carried out was Samuel Colson, who was from Newcastle upon Tyne. Before his execution he managed to write a note inside a prayer book, which was passed to an unnamed man who was serving the Dutch. From there the note was sown inside a mattress and passed through hands before making it to an Englishman named Mr Welden. This is an extract:

We were forced to confess that which we never knew, by reason of torment which flesh and blood were not able to endure. One by one (amongst which I was one) being ordered to confess or else endure the torments; and withal compelled Mr. Johnson who was before tormented, to witness against me, or else he should be tormented again which rather than he would endure, he said what they desired, he would speak; then I obliged to confess what I never knew, or else go to the torments, which rather than I would suffer.

In total ten Englishmen, nine Japanese and one Portuguese man were killed. When word reached England the whole country was shocked and enraged, demanding action be taken. Both countries put out propaganda leaflets to persuade people to believe their side of the events and the relationship between the two countries deteriorated. Eventually some compensation was paid to the families of those murdered, however I am unable to confirm if the family of Samuel Colson received any.

THE VICTORIA HALL STAMPEDE

The tragic event that took place in Victoria Hall in Sunderland on 16 June 1883 resulted in the deaths of 183 children.

A group of travelling entertainers had put on a show and at the end promised children with a certain number on their ticket a prize, causing a rush to the stage.

At the bottom of the staircase, the door opened inward and had been bolted so as to leave a gap only wide enough for one child to pass at a time. It is believed this was to ensure orderly checking of tickets. Those at the front were crushed to death by the weight of those behind them. One survivor, William Codling Jr, recalled:

> Soon we were most uncomfortably packed but still going down. Suddenly I felt that I was treading upon someone lying on the stairs and I cried in horror to those behind 'Keep back, keep back! There's someone down.' It was no use, I passed slowly over and onwards with the mass and before long I passed over others without emotion.

THE DEATH OF A CHIMNEY SWEEP

On the morning of Saturday, 28 September 1872, Thomas Clark, Gateshead chimney sweep, arrived at Washington New Hall in Sunderland with his young helper Christopher Drummond to begin the day's work. Sir Isaac Bell, Liberal Party politician and owner of

Washington New Hall, tasked Thomas with clearing the conservatory and fernery flues.

The job was going well until a blockage was located in one of the fernery flues. After persisting with a traditional brush, Thomas decided to send the young boy he had brought with him up to see if a stone was lodged. Christopher Drummond was 6 years old at the time and although the practice of using children as chimney sweeps had been outlawed, many still did it. During the Victorian era children were popularly used to clean chimneys due to their small size and ability to work in a confined space. Those who found themselves in this unfortunate career often had short lifespans due to the constant inhalation of soot and accidents such as falling from great heights.

After fifteen minutes Christopher did not return and his master concluded the boy was taking a nap, so a makeshift tool was fashioned to prod him. When no response came, a young lad named Winter from the village climbed up and tried to free Christopher, who was gasping for air. Unable to wrestle him free, a rope was passed around his legs and he was pulled out. To everyone's horror, the young man had died trapped in the chimney, and though he was rushed to the Crossed Keys Inn in an attempt to revive him it was unsuccessful.

In 1873, Thomas Clark was charged with manslaughter and found guilty, being sentenced to six months in prison with hard labour. At the trial the judge told him: 'I trust this will be a warning to you and others to abandon the cruel and barbarous practice of sending young boys into chimneys.'

SEABURN ZOO

For anyone who has visited the beautiful shores of Seaburn, the idea that a stone's throw from the amusements once sat a large zoo is an idea foreign to most. Changing owners and exhibits, the large zoo once hosted dolphins, bears, crocodiles, monkeys, lions and tigers. At a time when our social conscience was not what it is today, no one batted an eyelid at the thought of keeping these magnificent exotic beasts on the cold North East coast in habitats that were by today's standards more than below par.

While there are many tales I have heard from this particular zoo over the years, such as escaped lions getting into the cemetery and refuse from an abattoir being used to feed the animals, none stands out more than the case of Janet Coghlan, then Davidson.

At the age of 12, Janet had the opportunity to work in the zoo, doing various jobs to help with the upkeep of the establishment under the ownership of Martin Lacey. I think it is a fair assessment to say most young people would jump at the chance to be so close to such beautiful exotic animals and care for their wellbeing, while getting to see the joy they bring to others. With this job, however, came an element of danger and Janet was soon subject to this.

One day Janet was tasked with cleaning out the enclosure of Meena the tiger, a duty she had done previously without trouble. This time, however, things were different and while going to perform her duties the tiger leapt up and clawed at her face. The rapid attack, which may well have been the tiger's attempt at being playful, was ceased when other members of staff quickly intervened, but not before her face and neck were ripped open. The result was that Janet needed more than 200 stitches in her face, being later compensated with only a bar of chocolate for the incident. The zoo did not last long after this and was closed shortly after with many of the animals being moved to other locations for exhibition.

Lacey also owned an indoor zoo in Newcastle's Bigg Market, where there were jaguars and giraffes kept in the bustling heart of the city for people to look at. One story tells how a keeper would walk one of the jaguars down the street, turning heads as he went, perhaps to help build publicity for the attraction, but this zoo also did not have a long existence.

While the idea of inner city and coastal zoos up here in the North East now seem foreign and a distant memory, I think it is important to understand that they were a product of their time. When there was little health and safety, and animals were thought of as a novelty and not in the terms we understand them now, there were locations like ours all over the country, often having their own tales of mishaps and accidents sometimes resulting in a fatality. Thankfully attitudes have changed and more efforts are being made to preserve these creatures in the wild.

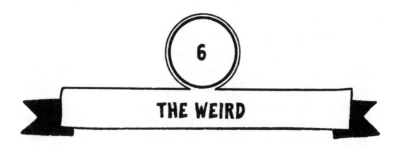

THE WEIRD

Our fascination with the unexplainable permeates into every part of our culture, spreading throughout history like an uncontrollable virus. It passes the mouths of those sat round campfires and into the wanting ears of the desperate who too want to believe in something more. In our little section of England we have encountered more than our share of the bizarre and weird, and this catalogue will showcase some of the stories that you yourself may want to tell on a dark night.

MASS EXECUTION OF WITCHES

During the seventeenth century the witch hunt craze spread across England, with women and occasionally men being accused of having a partnership with the devil and practising the dark arts. Following a brief occupation by Scottish forces, justice in Newcastle was left to the Puritan Corporation. For those familiar with the history of witchcraft and its more infamous instances, you may see a connection here as it was also the Puritans who played a hand in the notorious Salem witch trials in North America, where the corpses of some of the accused were burned after they were found guilty of witchcraft-related crimes.

While many assume burning witches was indeed the common form of punishment for dealing with those accused of this crime, in England that was simply not the case – most were hanged. The Newcastle witch trials took place in the same period as the infamous Witchfinder General Matthew Hopkins, who travelled up and down the country being paid for his services of outing witches and seeing them punished. Although it is not thought to be Hopkins himself who was brought in to test the victims' supernatural talents, one Witchfinder did visit Newcastle following a series of paranoid accusations.

Contrary to another popular belief that witches were thrown into water to see if they would float, the methodology used here was pricking the bare skin of the accused to see if it would draw blood, as well as searching for the devil's mark on the body. From simple revenge to genuine belief, numerous people found guilty were brought to the Town Moor with their fate sadly decided. Without anything to confess, fourteen women and one man met the hangman's noose under the belief they were children of the devil in what is considered one of the largest mass executions of witches in England. Such notions may seem bizarre and unrelatable today, but in certain corners of the world there are still those accused of witchcraft who sadly suffer terrible consequences as a result.

ROMAN GIANT

In 1759, a 9½ft human skeleton was discovered near Fulwell lime quarries. A letter in the *Gentlemen's Magazine* of October 1763 gives an account of this gigantic human skeleton found on the Fulwell hills, together with two Roman coins:

A few weeks ago a gentleman from Durham shewed me some large teeth and two Roman coins. The teeth, he said, he took out of the jaw of a gigantic skeleton of a man, and the coins were found in the grave near it. The account he gives is in the substance as follows: Upon Fulwell hills, near Monk-Weremouth, within a measured mile of the sea, there are quarries of lime, which he rents of the proprietor. In the year 1759 he removed a ridge of lime-stone and rubbish upon one of these quarries, which was about twenty-five yards in length from East to West; its perpendicular height about a yard and a half, its breadth at the top was near six yards, and the sides were sloping like the ruins of a rampart. In the middle of this bank was found the skeleton of a human body, which measured nine feet six inches in length; the shin bone measuring two feet three inches from the knee to the ankle; the head lay to the West, and was defended from the superincumbent earth by four large flat stones, which the relater, a man of great probity, who was present when the skeleton was measured, and who himself took the teeth out of the jaw, saw removed. The coins were found on the South side of the skeleton, near the right hand. P. Collinson.

In 1820, a small statue dedicated to a Roman god was also found in a nearby quarry at Carley Hill. The small statue known as a Lar was of a kind often used to protect a house, a shrine at a crossroads or even a Roman family as they sat to dinner.

There is much debate about Sunderland's historic connection to Roman times, with numerous other coins and artefacts being discovered. Many believe the evidence points to a Roman fort once being a part of the city, although this remains unconfirmed.

ALIEN ABDUCTION

The story of the Gateshead Grey takes place during 1940 in Gateshead and is thought by some to be the first recorded case of an alien abduction in Great Britain.

Robert Hall, a local boy who was 5 at the time, was out with a friend watching soldiers march past Saltwell Road in the Bensham area of Gateshead. When returning to his home on Hedley Street, he encountered a strange craft surrounded by light. He describes seeing numerous aliens of different sizes gathered round, the majority of which were short and grey but one was said to look like Bigfoot. The creatures all spoke English and he remembers being taken onto the ship and having a blood sample taken from his neck.

The whole event was said to have lasted for twenty minutes before he was allowed to leave. When he arrived home he immediately informed his parents of the bizarre events. They did not believe him and told him to keep quiet, however the story doesn't end there. The next day two men in black suits came to his house and told him that if anything was said he would disappear.

A few days after this, while walking to the shop to get his father's paper, he was chased up a back lane by another grey alien. In his own words, 'As I screamed me Uncle Ernie smashed it's heed in with a shovel.'

Both were shocked by the now dead creature before them, and Robert's uncle sent him to Saltwell Road to get Police Sergeant Brooks. When he arrived on the scene the corpse was put into a coal sack and taken to St Cuthbert's Church on Bensham Road until the authorities could deal with it. It reportedly lay there for three months.

EGYPTIAN MUMMY

The Egyptian Mummies at the Hancock Museum in Newcastle have attracted generations of curious people to the exhibition. Perhaps part of the attraction was the rumours that the mummies would wander the building at night.

Bakt-en-Hor was the first of the two to be bought for the museum, having been donated to the Literary and Philosophical Society in 1821 and purchased by the Hancock when it opened in 1884. She is believed to be from between 1070 and 713 BC and to this day she has not been unwrapped, remaining in her original linen wrappings.

Irtryu, the second mummy, was presented to the Newcastle Literary and Philosophical Society in 1826 after being bought from an auction of the collection of Baron Dominique Vivant Denon. Baron Denon collected the mummy in Egypt in 1789–90 when he was part of the scholarly expedition that accompanied Napoleon's campaign and it is believed to date from 664–525 BC. The unwrapped blackened remains and the unusual choice to display the body upright once made it a popular attraction.

Since they have been housed in the museum there have been reports of noises in the building at night and alarms going off in their exhibition. It was also said Irtryu's hand would always end up on the floor somehow despite being securely fastened numerous times. Superstitions surrounding mummies are still prevalent in popular culture today.

DINOSAUR BONE

In 2011, a man walked into the Winter Gardens in Sunderland with a bag containing a piece of vertebra that once belonged to an Iguanodon. The 130-million-year-old bone had been uncovered by a member of the public while they were digging among tree roots in their garden.

The bone is the only find of its kind in the area as dinosaur bones are younger than the rocks here. The region is on the Permian strata, which is 250 million years old, and this makes it unlikely the bone originated here.

The Iguanodon was first recognised by British paleontologist Gideon Mantell in the 1800s. Fossils like this have frequently been found on the south-east coast of England, meaning it is possibly a souvenir that has made its way up the country, or another explanation would be that it is a seemingly unique case of glacial transport. The bone is currently on display in the Winter Gardens in Sunderland.

MYSTERY LIGHTS

Throughout history there are many recorded cases of unexplainable lights being seen by multiple witnesses. Sometimes these lights appear in the sky or the wilderness but in the instance of the Whitburn Lights, also known as the Durham Lights, they appeared to those who were nearby at sea and lured their ships to be wrecked.

Charles Fort, world-renowned investigator of the paranormal and inspiration behind the *Fortean Times*, researched the phenomena. In his book *The Book of the Damned* (1919), he had this to say:

Every now and then in the English newspapers, in the middle of the nineteenth century, there is something about lights that were seen against the sky, but as if not far above land, oftenest upon the coast of Durham. They were mistaken for beacons by sailors. Wreck after wreck occurred. The fishermen were accused of displaying false lights and profiting by wreckage. The fishermen answered that mostly only old vessels, worthless except for insurance, were so wrecked.

During a ten-year period from 1860, more than 150 ships were wrecked on the rocks near Whitburn after being lured by a light or lights above land that their crews wrongly believed were from a lighthouse at the mouth of the Tyne. This led to local fishermen being accused of luring the ships to be wrecked and then looting their cargo.

The government intervened after Durham MP Sir Hedworth Williamson tabled questions in the House of Commons. In December 1865, a commission of inquiry led by Rear Admiral Sir Richard Collinson travelled to Sunderland to investigate. The lights were described as very mysterious, but perhaps more interestingly as a result of this inquiry the government approved the building of Souter Point Lighthouse. Its opening in 1871 put an end to the phenomena.

FLYING SAUCERS

In December 1964, an article was published in Ray Palmer's American magazine *Flying Saucers* relating to an experience in Leam Lane, Gateshead, that could be described as out of this world. The article was written by Harry Lord, a member of the Tynedale UFO society, and details multiple testimonies from people in the area who had seen the phenomenon.

At 11:35 p.m. on 31 May 1964, it was reported that the Bell family of Gateshead saw three luminous egg-shaped objects pass through the sky from east to west. The same night almost an hour later neighbours were awoken by a loud humming noise that lasted thirty minutes. The noise was said to sound like 'a swarm of bees, but approximately twenty times louder'.

The article reports that on 2 June 1964 David Wilson, aged 14, went to Leam Lane Farm, where he encountered a group of roughly ten 'children' who stood within approximately 20m of him on a haystack. As he approached, he saw human beings of a size of 6ft or 8½ft who stood two by two on the haystack. They were in green costumes, with 'hands that seemed to be like lit electric bulbs'. They were digging through the haystack as if they were looking for something.

Other testimonies in the article include a young girl saying that their chief 'was dressed in black and carried a stick with pink lines'. Another girl allegedly saw one of the humanoids sitting on the roof of a barn. Other children claimed that they had observed a dwarf who was riding on the back of a cow. A girl observed a circular silver object of the size of a car take off in a rotational movement and release an orange gleam.

Flying Saucers magazine and Ray Palmer are both known for sensationalising stories and hold little in the way of credibility. That being said, it would not be the first time aliens are reported to have visited Gateshead.

LOCH NESS MONSTER

Beginning in the sixth century, recorded sightings of the legendary Scottish creature known as the Loch Ness Monster date back hundreds of years. A number of those sightings have been proved fake and definitive proof of its existence has yet to be presented. Unlike the iconic Surgeons Photograph that most associate with Nessie, this one, taken by a local man from Gateshead, was quickly forgotten about.

Peter O'Connor was an ex-Royal Marine and former fireman living in Gateshead in 1960 at the time of his encounter with the reclusive creature. Alongside another local man named Fred Fulcher, from Hebburn, the two set off up north. Roughly a mile north-east of Foyers Bay on the Loch, in the early hours of the morning, the two men caught sight of Nessie swimming. In this quote from a letter Peter wrote as a contribution for a book titled *The Loch Ness Monster*, he recounts his experience:

Between 0600–0630 hours I left the camp (1 mile N.E. of Foyers Bay) and went N.E. for 100 yards. The Loch Ness Monster glided around the headland at a fast walking pace. I waded into the water to get as close to the route it intended passing as possible. I was waist deep and decided to go no closer as it had turned its head in my direction and I am sure it knew I was there. For a moment (a horrible one) I thought it intended coming towards me. I watched its head closely.

It had small sheep-like features set on a very, very, strong neck – the muscles kept rippling in it, reminding me of a panther's leg when pacing a cage. The head was approx. 10 inches long, the neck 6–7 inches in diameter increasing in thickness towards water – there was 2–3ft exposed and behind the neck was a large hump or body, greyish-black in colour. Where I expected limbs (i.e. Plesiosaurus) I saw the occasional swirl of water indicating them. I saw no eyes, but its facial structure suggests it has them, but its 'lids' were shut. The skin appeared smooth, as on a seal, but could have been fine scale.

Following this, Peter took the photograph, which is available to view online should you look hard enough. The creature is said to have been startled by this and disappeared to the murky depths below with haste. Shortly after these events the story and Peter's account made headline news but disappeared quickly.

SOMNAMBULISM

Somnambulism, or sleepwalking as it is commonly known today, is a condition that often led to newsworthy stories in 1800s. Throughout history there have been examples of sleeping people doing strange things from murder to mischief. This section recalls some local stories that made it into the newspapers more than one hundred years ago.

The *Jarrow Express* reported in 1891 two stories relating to this unusual condition. Early in the morning, a man was walking along Grange Road when he happened to come across a woman seemingly walking around in her sleep. He watched the woman cross the road, when she stumbled and awoke, giving her a terrible fright. When the man went to her assistance it emerged that she had walked from her home near Hill Street entirely unconscious of the fact.

In 1894 the *Shields Gazette* reported that a young man in Sunderland had tried to leave his residence by climbing up the chimney. When this became too difficult he opened a window, climbed onto the roof, and leapt over to the next building along. He then climbed down the drainpipe to be greeted by a policeman, who woke him up. It was later revealed that the young man was on holiday and had been dreaming of his home in Hartlepool.

It seems sleepwalking was often a very dangerous condition, with people frequently injuring themselves. The *Newcastle Guardian* and *Tyne Mercury* reported in 1869 that a Henry Finlay's night-time excursion had fatal consequences. It is said his brother did not notice anything strange about Henry when he went to sleep this night and only by chance noticed he was not in his bed. Realising Henry's clothes were by the bed, he then began to search for him. Henry was discovered in the back garden floating in a shallow pond, where it appears he had drowned after walking into it while sleepwalking.

The *Newcastle Journal* published a story in 1895 that describes another local fatality. Robert Reynolds, a crane man residing in Tyneside Terrace, had retired to bed early one Saturday night. Hearing some disturbance from the room, his friends went to check on him only to see Robert in the process of climbing out of his bedroom window. Unable to save him, he fell from the second storey and died a few days later from his injuries.

While sleepwalking is generally more common in children, cases of this condition deemed newsworthy seem a lot less frequent. How strange it must have been to have witnessed one of these nocturnal wanderers in the early hours of the morning on an empty street.

PREHISTORIC WEARSIDE

In 1911 an ancient burial ground was discovered within a barrow on Hastings Hill in Sunderland. Discovered and excavated by two men, Dr C. Greenwell and C. T. Trenchmann, the funerary monument is said to date back to 2,000 BC. Aside from Greenwell's suspicions about the mound, another reason for their interest dates back to a record of an incident that took place on 5 October 1827.

The discovery of a skeleton in the area, recorded as still having hair on its head, shocked local residents, who believed a murder had occurred. It was later concluded that while the skeleton was human, the hair believed to have been attached to it was more likely to be roots from a nearby plant that had grown through the skull. This record alongside Greenwell's suspicions led to him contacting the landowner, Mr Brown, who agreed to let the excavation take place.

In early November 1911 the excavation took place, and inside the barrow an area roughly 12m in diameter and 1m high was found. This chamber-like monument was built into the limestone of the hill and most likely covered with earth and rubble. Inside the tomb were found a number of human skeletal remains of men, a woman and a child. Highly decorated clay utensils were also uncovered along with animal remains such as a pig's tooth and antlers from a stag, all most likely left with them for their journey into the unknown. It was reported that the remains of ten people were found, six of whom were cremated while the others were not.

The remains are housed in Sunderland Museum and Winter Gardens but one of the city's most important historic sites is now largely forgotten. The question of what made these hunter-gatherers from Wearside important enough to receive such a burial will remain unanswered. From the vantage point of Hastings Hill ancient man would have looked out across forests inhabited by wolves, deer and wild boar, which is something quite different from what you see from there today.

WIZARD OF THE NORTH

Said to have been born in the border regions of Scotland or Northern England in the thirteenth century, Michael Scott would live a life steeped in myth and legend. While little is known about his early years, he is reported to have been devoted to his study of mathematics, astrology, philosophy and theology. Studying at Oxford University, then moving to Paris, as he travelled his reputation spread rapidly and led to him tutoring the pope and become astrologer to Frederick II, the Holy Roman Emperor.

Many tales of his powers have survived to this day and he is often recognised as one of Great Britain's most well-documented magical figures. He is said to have turned witches to stone in Cumbria, split the Eildon Hills into three sections in Melrose and made rope from sand in Fife.

One story closer to home tells how Scott arrived in Morpeth and was welcomed with a feast. The people of the town discussed in private what to ask the infamous sorcerer, and decided they would urge him to bring the tide an additional 5 miles up the River Wansbeck to allow them to have a port to economically compete with Newcastle. The wizard granted their request and delegated a servant to carry out his instructions the following morning. Large crowds formed in the neighbourhood of Cambois to watch Scott perform his spells. Huge waves were said to form as the servant ran, instructed not to look behind him, leading the tide up the river. As the waves gathered in pace and strength, the servant could not resist looking behind, only to have the tide lose its momentum immediately, denying the people of Morpeth their wish. In Durham, Scott was said to have conducted a similar ritual with the River Wear in an attempt to bring it to the city.

Another gift Scott possessed was that of prophecy. The legendary sorcerer accurately predicted a number of future events and foretold his own death. He envisioned a small pebble falling from the sky and hitting him in the head, killing him. To prevent this he wore a metal cap to protect his head, only taking it off while in church, and it was coming out of church that a pebble did indeed hit him in the head. While it is said he did not die immediately, his health deteriorated quickly and he did so soon after.

Fibonacci, believed to have been a student of Scott's, dedicated the second version of his famous book on mathematics, *Liber Abaci*, to him. Scott is also immortalised in Dante's *Inferno*, where he appears in the eighth circle of hell.

STRANDED IN ICE

Sir Richard Collinson was an English naval officer and explorer who was born in Gateshead in 1811. At age 12, Richard joined the Royal Navy and steadily rose through its ranks, reaching captain by 1842. In his early years he served in the first opium war in China and surveyed its coast, producing charts on which all its successors were based.

In 1845, fellow member of the Royal Navy and explorer John Franklin began an Arctic expedition to charter the unexplored coastline. Franklin, who was 59 at the time, set off with HMS *Erebus* and HMS *Terror* in the hope of documenting the dangerous terrain. The two ships would disappear in the Canadian Arctic along with their crew after it is believed they became trapped in the ice. Two years passed and Franklin's wife urged the Admiralty to send out a search party to find her husband, who had left with three years of food supplies. The Admiralty waited another year before launching a new search and offered a reward of £20,000 to find the expedition.

One of those tasked with finding Franklin was Richard Collinson, who in 1850 set off on HMS *Enterprise* accompanied by Robert McClure commanding HMS *Investigator*. Collinson continued along to the coast of Victoria Island, where in 1853 he led a sledge party to the easternmost point. It was here an Inuit drew a map of an area to the east that contained a ship. If Collinson had not disregarded this, or perhaps had a more competent interpreter, he might have sent a sledge party east and found Franklin's men if any of them had survived. In 1854, while surveying for the Hudson Bay Company, a Scottish man called Dr John Rae is believed to have uncovered the fate of those on board *Erebus* and *Terror*. His report to the Admiralty consisted of interviews with Inuit hunters, who described how the ships had become icebound and conditions were so dire the men had succumbed to the cold and even cannibalism. Lady Franklin was enraged by this and her desperation for answers would lead to a further twenty-five searches over the next four decades.

The mystery of what happened to Franklin and his 129 crew members continues to capture the imagination of people today. Searches of the area over the years have uncovered the bodies of those believed to have been on board the ships, some of which show signs of cannibalism. Richard Collinson is often overlooked as an explorer, as Robert McClure, who arrived first, has received most of the recognition. It is hard to say if Collinson had investigated the ship on the map whether things would have turned out differently, but what is known is the tragic effect of the disappearance of *Erebus* and *Terror*.

The story of HMS *Terror* was recently told in a fictionalised dramatisation produced by another local legend, director Sir Ridley Scott, who was born in South Shields. Did he know of our local connection to this harrowing story?

WALLSEND WITCH

This interesting tale of witchcraft in the North East is alleged to have taken place in Wallsend many years ago. While the specific date of this event is unknown, the story is believed to have originated from Sir Francis Blake Delaval, who was alive during the 1700s and had heard it from another source. It was later published in the *Monthly Chronicle of North-Country Lore and Legend* in 1888 as well as the *Local Historian's Table Book* by M.A. Richardson.

Our story begins with an adventurer returning from Newcastle after nightfall when he happened to pass an old church, likely the Holy Cross Church, only to see it lit up. Leaving his servant with the horses, he crept inside and spotted a grizzly sight through the window. Inside were a circle of hags surrounding the corpse of a young woman, illuminated by a fire burning brightly within a skull sat nearby.

Watching a shocking scene unfold, he witnessed one of the withered hags sever the left breast of the deceased woman. The dissector, described as having a stubbly beard, buck teeth, red fiery eyes and withered wrinkled skin, then passed the body part to her companion, who left in the direction of the belfry. Unafraid, the man burst in determined to make the hags pay for their foul crimes, only for a number of them to disappear through the roof and windows. Somehow the adventurer grabbed the one responsible for desecrating the corpse and restrained her using a handkerchief in his possession to tie her hands.

Making haste, he left with his servant, determined to see justice for the evil deeds he had witnessed on holy ground. Here there is a gap in the story as where her trial was held, if she had one, is unknown, but for her punishment it was decided to burn her at the stake. This quote from *Monthly Chronicle* describes the final scene:

And now followed the most marvellous part of the story – so marvellous, indeed, that we must beg our readers to take it, as we ourselves do, with a grain of salt. When the sentence was about to be carried into execution, the witch requested to have the use of two new wooden dishes, which were forthwith procured from the neighbouring hamlet of Seaton Sluice. The wood and combustibles were then heaped on the sands, the culprit was placed thereon, the dishes were given to her, and fire was applied to the pile. As the smoke arose in dense columns around her, she placed a foot in each of the utensils, muttered a spell, cleared herself from the fastenings at the stake, and soared away on the sea-breeze like an eagle escaped from the hands of its captors. But when she had risen to a considerable height, one of the dishes which supported her lost its efficacy from having been, by the young person who procured them, dipped unthinkingly in pure fresh water; and so, after making several gyrations, the deluded follower of Satan fell to the ground. Without affording her another chance of escape, the beholders conveyed her back to the pile, where she perished amidst its flames.

The burning of witches in England was an uncommon practice, with the punishment for those deemed guilty often being hanging such as the infamous witch trials of Newcastle in the 1600s. While this story is likely a fabrication, it is another great example of a dark piece of folklore from our North East.

MESMERISM AND HYPNOSIS

Mesmerism, also known as hypnotism, was a popular Victorian era stage attraction. During the 1800s, increasing amounts of performers claiming to have mesmerising powers began putting on shows before packed theatre halls. The performance itself would often consist of the host putting people into a trance and making them do strange things, such as believe they were on a wrecked ship or that they were a chicken, however the shows would sometimes be more diverse. Many performers claimed clairvoyant abilities and would put their partner into a mesmerised trance, making them draw a person they had never seen before or describe facts from the person's life.

These mysterious powers seem widely accepted at the time and as such were used for a number of different purposes. One article from 1866 describes how a North Shields man named Mr Hansen was honoured by the community for his use of mesmeric powers. For a number of years Hansen had used mesmerism to cure people of toothache for free and as a reward was gifted a portrait from a number of grateful locals.

The visit of a mesmerist named Mr Morgan to South Shields in 1861 reportedly had a troubling effect on a number of youths. Inspired by the forces they had witnessed, one young man invited two friends over when his parents were out to try his own hand at using the enigmatic force. When touching his friends' heads, the participant snapped, attacking his two friends and smashing himself through the window. Having eventually been caught, the temporarily maddened young man calmed down, but the article warns of the potentially fatal consequences of experimenting with the unknown.

The final tale of mesmeric madness is perhaps the most strange of all. An article from the *Newcastle Chronicle* in 1868 describes how a young sailor was drinking at the Ferry Hotel in Sunderland when he was approached by a strange man named Mckenzie, who performed some mesmeric passes on him. The extremely susceptible sailor went into a coma-like state under the complete control of the mysterious stranger he had just met at the bar. Mckenzie later took the man outside to revive him, then departed, leaving the sailor in a bizarre state. Having been brought to bed by his friends, the man woke the next day still feeling the effects of what had been done to him. He was then taken to Monkwearmouth to see another mesmerist, who was unfortunately not home. On their return home his behaviour continued to be erratic and he climbed onto the roof of a two-storey building, an action believed to have been ordered by Mckenzie the night before, and refused to come down. When he was eventually coaxed down he was committed to the workhouse until it could be figured out what to do. The police tracked down Mckenzie, who initially denied any knowledge but eventually caved and agreed to come with the police to restore the man's state of mind. However, when Mckenzie arrived at the workhouse the sailor was too medicated to speak to and it is unknown if he regained his wits.

ANGOLA'S MIGHTY CZAR OF ALL LION TAMERS

Martini Maccomo was an African lion tamer believed to have been born between 1835 and 1840. Little is known about his early life but Maccomo was said to have been born in Angola before making his way to the United States of America, where he toured with Stone & McCollum's circus. In 1861 he had made it to England and was performing with William Manders' Menagerie, where he was billed as 'Angola's Mighty Czar of All Lion Tamers', drawing large crowds.

William Manders' Menagerie was the first to bring exotic animals like elephants, camels and monkeys to much of the British public for the first time, although many came just to see the lion tamer. Maccomo used whips, pistols and knuckledusters to keep the animals under control at his shows, but this could lead to accidents. At Greenwich Fair in 1857, while being attacked by a lion, Maccomo shot his pistol into the audience by mistake. This resulted in a piece of wadding being lodged in the eye of a local carpenter, who was awarded £150 in damages.

It seems Maccomo frequently had accidents in the ring, more often than not resulting in him being mauled. At a show in Liverpool in 1861 Maccomo's hand became lodged in the mouth of a Bengal tigress for more than five minutes until another keeper pressed a hot iron bar against its teeth to free him. While in Norwich in 1862, he lost part of his finger after being dragged around the ring by the lion, who had bitten into his hand.

Maccomo arrived in Sunderland with William Manders' Menagerie in 1869. While performing he was attacked by a lion named Wallace and badly injured. The lion remained with the group of performers and Maccomo recovered, continuing their tour. Maccomo returned to Sunderland two years later, however this time he caught rheumatic fever and became sick. The infamous lion tamer had survived numerous bouts in the ring against deadly beasts but it was the illness that ended up claiming his life in the Palatine Hotel in Sunderland.

He is buried in Bishopwearmouth Cemetery in the Commonwealth graves section under a headstone erected by William Manders. Wallace the lion outlived Maccomo by four years and after its death was purchased by the Sunderland Museum and Winter Gardens, where it is still on display today.

ELEPHANT ON TRIAL

Mademoiselle D'Jeck was a performing Siamese elephant who made her theatre debut in Paris in 1829. The successful performance saw her travel to London later that same year, where she starred in *The Elephant of Siam and the Fire Fiend*, which ran until April the following year. Shortly after this, D'Jeck travelled to Edinburgh to perform at a theatre and following this was scheduled to travel by boat to Tyneside for a performance at Newcastle. However, due to rough conditions at sea she began a long walk instead.

D'Jeck made the walk with her entourage without being led by a rope and on the way made a stop in Morpeth. Although D'Jeck was said not to have a violent nature it was here that she killed her keeper, Jean Baptiste. It is believed Jean aggravated the elephant by striking it and as a resulted was crushed to death by the elephant's trunk. When the performer reached Newcastle, a trip that took a total of four days from Edinburgh, she was put on trial. Despite her crime she had still been booked to perform at the Theatre Royal on Mosley Street and was fined 5s for the incident. This amount could be considered a small sum as she was reportedly paid £20 per performance, but it is believed Jean's previous cruelty to the animal allowed her some leniency. The Theatre Royal had to have the stage door specially widened for the large Miss D'Jeck, however it seems to have been worth it as the performance was a success.

Shortly after her appearance at Newcastle she travelled to America and performed in New York, although her stay was short and she returned to England in July 1831. Her return unfortunately saw another incident take place where she was reported to have half-killed a baker before she travelled to France and killed a man in Bordeaux. In another incident she was said to have broken her keeper's arm in two places, and while in Bavaria set fire to her shed.

The larger-than-life performer met an unfortunate end when in Geneva she broke a priest's ribs, resulting in an order that she be killed. After attempts at shooting her did not end her life, she was shot with a cannonball fired from a circus cannon and the meat from her body was sold for eating. Mademoiselle D'Jeck no doubt endured much cruelty in her life but also brought joy to many and is certainly one elephant the world will never forget.

THE BRITISH BAN ON HORROR COMICS

Comic strips have long been a part of British society, spanning the Penny Dreadfuls of the nineteenth century to the iconic local *Viz*. Following the Second World War, American comic strips began to make their way across the water and into the hands of British children. Comics like *Tales from the Crypt* and the *Vault of Horror* were more violent and shocking than anything seen in England before and young people all over the country were fascinated by them. This began to cause a moral panic across the nation as parents discovered the gruesome stories their children were reading.

In 1955 the Children and Young Persons (Harmful Publications) Act was passed specifically to deal with the horror comic issue. Popular South Shields MP James Ede was a strong supporter of the ban on such comics and held them responsible for corrupting Britain's youth: 'I say of the horror comic that it is evil absolutely; against manners in this country.'

Comics were still sold by backstreet newsagents who had imported blocks from the USA to print, but ultimately their popularity was crushed. Even before this Act came into effect there were prosecutions. It is reported that in 1953 a South Shields newsagent was brought before the local magistrates under obscene publications legislation and ordered to destroy 20,000 comics.

In 1969 the Act was made permanent and it continues to be in effect today, represented, for example, in the Royal Mail prohibition against mailing horror comics and the matrices used to print them.

RAINING CATS AND DOGS - OR NOT?

Throughout time there have been rare occasions where the sky has opened up and dropped something other than water to the ground. One such occasion happened in Hendon, Sunderland, on 24 August 1918.

Surprised locals living between Commercial Road and the southern end of Canon Cockin Street witnessed the sight of hundreds of eels falling from the sky for ten minutes straight. Many of the eels were frozen solid and broke when they hit the ground.

This took place shortly after a fierce thunderstorm, which is believed to be the explanation.

ATLANTIS

The story you are about to read was originally published in *Fate Magazine* in February 1958 before later being published in a book titled *Out of Time and Place* some years later. While *Fate Magazine* is not exactly known as the most credible news source, what I found particularly interesting was the number of facts that could be easily verified. The story itself is more than seven pages long and what follows is the condensed version.

The Jesmond was a steam schooner launched on the Tyne in 1880. Not only did *The Jesmond* have a steam engine but also sails on three masts to take advantage of the wind, thus making it a fairly powerful ship. Captain David Amory Robson, from Jarrow, arrived in Messina, Sicily, in February 1882 and delivered his shipment of coal before cleaning out the hold and filling it with a cargo of dried apricots and prunes bound for New Orleans. It is thought that due to the speedy pace at which the ship had completed its journey, the turnaround was very quick and allowed it to continue its journey ahead of schedule. The plan was to arrive in New Orleans and pick up a cargo of cotton to return to Liverpool, although something odd happened on their journey.

While heading south to catch the strong trade winds, some 200 miles south of Madeira Cap the sea took on an unusual appearance. The water was murky, muddy and carpeted with dead fish as far as the eye could see. The date was roughly 1 March and it is reported a submarine volcanic eruption was responsible for the grand scale of carnage the crew of *The Jesmond* saw before them. Interestingly another ship, *The Westbourne* of Hull, was nearby, although this was before radio and the two ships could not communicate. Just after dawn, Captain Robson was awoken by his second officer following a declaration of land where records showed only 2,000 fathoms of water.

Luckily for the crew, they had arrived at this mysterious island at dawn rather than during the night when the ship might have run aground. Having been erected from the depths by the volcanic blast, an island now existed where one had not previously and was described as having lofty peaks wreathed in the volcanic smoke that birthed it. Due to the quick pace at which *The Jesmond* had performed its duties it was ahead of schedule and Captain Robson, seeing it as his duty to explore the island, now situated in the main shipping lane for ships bound for America from the Mediterranean, set course.

Hundreds of miles away from the nearest recorded land, they set off on a smaller boat to scramble up the cliffs of this newly discovered island. It was a barren, lifeless landscape, and the surface was so cut by fissures and chasms that the party decided to return to the beach and explore where they could hope to make better progress in the time available. One of the sailors, who had brought equipment to help climb the cliffs, stirred the loose gravel beneath him with one of the tools and unearthed flint arrowheads, creating an immediate buzz of excitement. The popularity of archaeology at the time was strongly associated with treasure hunting and the crew began searching with enthusiasm. More arrowheads were soon found as well as small knives but soon night fell and the crew returned to their ship determined to come back the following morning.

On their second venture to the island, with better equipment this time, the crew dug up a large stone statue encrusted with seashells thought to have lain on the seabed for a long time. Further relics were discovered including a metal sword, pottery, spearheads and jars containing bones. All of this was loaded onto the ship as the weather worsened and the crew set sail to their original destination. Looking out at the island for the last time (as it soon sank beneath the waves once more), it is highly unlikely Captain Robson thought of Plato's Atlantis, which was described as being very close to the coordinates of the island before them. Only a determined scholar could find reference to Atlantis at this time period and it was not until May later that year that the first edition of a bestselling book that publicised the idea of Atlantis would be published in England.

Upon arrival in New Orleans in March the story broke of the mystery island and the amazing finds the crew had recovered. The story was syndicated to more than a dozen North American newspapers with the original articles containing an offer to 'show the collection to any gentleman who was interested' and that Captain Robson would hand over the findings to the British Museum when he arrived in Liverpool. When the ship arrived back in their home country the collection did not make it into a British museum, however, and the entire crew kept their lips tightly sealed. One possible explanation is that some of it was sold due to the elemental value of some of the metals of the artefacts discovered, a private collector purchased all the finds, or that the entire story was a fake.

The writer of the story later published in the book mentioned above did some digging himself and raised some interesting points. The speed of the journey and turnaround allowed no time to collect fake materials, and as the statue alone weighed a ton it was unlikely to have been brought from Newcastle. Another observation was that the sighting of the island and result of the submarine volcanic eruption was corroborated by another ship with a British captain who docked in a different port on the same day, so it is difficult to believe that a practical joke could have been coordinated between the two in a time without radio. Were the crew asked to keep quiet in return for a share of the sale of its finds?

Captain Robson continued to captain the ship until 1884 and *The Jesmond* survived the First World War, only to be sold to the Japanese in 1925 after a number of refurbishments. The questions remain, however: did a man from the North East of England stumble across the lost city of Atlantis or was the story an elaborate fake? Do the artefacts from the expedition to the mystery island still exist as part of a family heirloom or private collection hidden away somewhere or have they been lost to time? Are there any living relatives of Captain Robson who have had the story told through the generations and know the truth to it all?

It is likely we will never know, that is unless Atlantis resurfaces again …

THE DEVIL HIMSELF

What you are about to read is a direct relaying, in olde English, of the appearance of Satan himself in Newcastle. It is sourced from *Memorials, or the memorable things that fell out within this island of Britain from 1638–1684* by Robert Law:

> Apryle 1672, there was a ship lying at Newcastle, bound for London, called the Good Hope of London, wherein the divill appeared in bodily shape, in the habit of a seaman, with a blew gravatt about his neck, and desired the master of the ship to remove out of her, which he did not obey, till sic time as she began to sink into the ocean. Then he, with his company, took his cog-boat, who were saved by another ship coming by, and that ship fyred and sank. This was testified by the oaths of them that were in her. They could never get ruther stir'd, nor use of the pump, an ominous presage.

There you have it, an account of the devil himself in Tyne and Wear. Was this a simple case of superstition or did the sailors indeed encounter the dark lord on this fateful night?

7

THINGS THAT GO BUMP IN THE NIGHT

When a person hears the word 'ghost' it often conjures up the image of someone in a white bedsheet with two ragged holes poked through for eyes. For others, however, their feelings and the image in their mind might relate back to a more personal experience they've had with *the other side*. Whether you are a believer or not, stories of life beyond the grave have permeated popular culture for decades, seeping into literature and cinema alike. The following stories relate to our varied experiences in the North East, with tales of the more well-known spooks to some that have been forgotten by the ages.

GHOSTS ON THE SHORE

You do not have to look far from Northern shores before you begin finding stories of noises in deep dark caves that dot our coast. One of the more well-known cases of ghostly goings on can be found in Marsden Grotto, South Shields, where its reputation has drawn in paranormal investigators from all over the country. The gruesome end of John the Jibber is just one such story that illustrates the wealth of history found in this particular location. Said to have been part of a group of smugglers, John the Jibber was one day found to have been betraying his fellow criminals by selling information to HM Customs.

Betrayed by a man they thought was an ally, the group sought revenge and caught John to deal out a harsh punishment. The story goes that he was stuffed into a barrel and left in a cave near to the Marsden Grotto's lift shaft and abandoned, alone in the dark, to starve to death. It is thought John the Jibber is just one of many spirits who dwell here.

Travelling further south to Sunderland you will find Roker Park a stone's throw away from the nearby beach. As you walk down the path through the park you will see a collection of caves, now largely sealed to the public, where it is thought another ghost resides named Spottee. As described by Alan Tedder in his book *Ghosts, Mysteries and Legends of Sunderland,* Spottee was a seaman hermit who earned his nickname from the spotted shirt he wore. Believed to have lived in one of these caves many years ago, Spottee was a sailor who had been shipwrecked and had made his home here. His inability to speak English led many to believe he was in fact mad, leading him to earn a living foraging and by begging. When he eventually passed away in the dark dwelling he called home the stories people told about his spirit were divided. Some say that he could be seen on stormy nights warning ships away from the jagged rocks that brought him here, while others say he lured them on to them to suffer the same tragic fate as he did.

In a now inaccessible cave hidden beneath Tynemouth Castle is a cavern once known as the Jingling Man's Hole. Similar to the legend of Spottee, the man who made use of this cave would gain his reputation by luring ships on to the rocks by planting lanterns, giving the appearance of safely docked ships along the coast of Tynemouth. When the ships were wrecked he would plunder the goods and stash them in the labyrinth of tunnels beneath the castle. It is said the jingling was a sound produced by shackles still wrapped around his legs, a sound that some say can still be heard on dark foggy nights from the nearby cliffs.

THE VIKING

One of the most well-known tales from the Tynemouth area is perhaps also one of the oldest. Dating back to the days of the Vikings, we begin with a raiding party beaching in Tynemouth to pillage what goods they could. After what is described as a disastrous venture, one of the lead Vikings named Olaf was wounded and left for dead by his comrades. The nearby monks of Tynemouth Priory happened across this injured invader and took pity on him, bringing him to the priory, where over time he was nursed back to health. Whether it was because of his gratitude to the monks, or his isolated existence, it is not known why Olaf eventually converted to Christianity. Taking his vows and joining the order, he would watch out to sea, fearful of another raid by his kinsmen.

It is not known exactly how long after this that day came, but Olaf spotted the Viking ships returning to plunder once more. Rumour has it that upon seeing this he went to the shrine of St Oswin to pray for deliverance from the threat while the monks manned their defences. Not wanting to be caught off guard again, they were prepared for the Vikings this time and refused the demand of the treasure held within the priory. A fierce clash took place, with the attackers being surprised by the resistance they faced. They retreated back to their boats to find an easier target, leaving behind the dead and wounded. Soon after the monks brought the corpses and the wounded men back to their infirmary, where Olaf was summoned.

When he arrived he recognised a familiar face among the deceased layed out before him. There, cold and lifeless, was the body of his brother Eric, who had been slain in the skirmish. Inconsolable with grief, Olaf returned to the shrine to be alone with his thoughts. Eventually the monks grew concerned for their convert and, entering the shrine, they saw him dead before the altar. Like many stories of coastal folklore, people say you can see him on windy days watching for the Viking ships on the horizon. While I cannot attest to the truth of this account, it is a popular story that continues to live on in the region to this day.

THE SPIRITS PHOTOGRAPH

James Dickinson was a photographer in Newcastle who owned a popular studio on Grainger Street during the 1800s. One Saturday morning a customer came in to enquire about a portrait of himself that had been taken in December. The man, who announced he was named J. T. Thompson, confirmed enough information that, although he didn't have a receipt, the photographer was satisfied with his identity and asked him to call back in an hour when his assistant was present.

Thompson became irate at this point and wearily explained he had been travelling all night and could not call again. Dickinson could see the man did not look well and tried his best to arrange a compromise but the man stormed out of the shop without a reply.

When the assistant arrived at the studio, Dickinson explained the events of the day, only for her to explain to him that a man claiming to be the man's father had come to the shop only a few days before requesting the photograph. The assistant had explained that they were behind on their work and it would not be ready for another week. Deciding Thompson had waited long enough, they searched through the pile of negatives to find the one of the man who visited the shop that morning so work could begin.

Six days later, Thompson's father returned to the shop to see if the work had been completed. During their discussion it was revealed that on the day of his son's supposed visit to the studio he had in fact been unconscious for the entire day up until his death at 2.30 p.m. The father went on to explain that his son had been calling out repeatedly for the photograph in the night, while in a delirious state, but was physically unable to leave the house and was surrounded by family.

The written records of who had visited the store and when, combined with the testimony of witnesses, left no doubt in the minds of those involved that J. T. Thompson had been in the store that Saturday to pick up his photograph. Multiple witnesses also testify to being with the man on his deathbed during that time, also leaving both the family and photographer at a loss for an explanation of the unusual events.

The story was recorded by William T. Stead in his book *Real Ghost Stories*, in which he proposes this explanation:

> The only other hypothesis that can be brought forward is that someone personated Thompson. Against this we have the fact that Mr. Dickinson, who had never seen Thompson, recognised him immediately as soon as he saw the negative of his portrait.

Stead is an interesting character in himself and one born in the North East at Embleton, Northumberland. Credited with being a pioneer in the field of journalism, he wrote for the *Northern Echo* but became increasingly interested in spiritualism later in life. Stead's life would end with the sinking of RMS *Titanic*, having often stated to friends that he would die as a result of drowning. Ten years after this his daughter, Estelle, declared she had made contact with Stead via a medium and went on to publish a book on the subject.

GHOSTLY PROPHECY

Taking place in Sunderland in 1843, this tale of a message from beyond the grave attracted attention from newspapers all over the country. This quote from the *Kentish Independent* sets the scene:

> Sunderland is in an uproar about a ghost! A young mariner of the Myrtle, named Cairns, saw his sister's ghost at sea, and again, few nights ago, in his vessel on the Wear. On the latter occasion she promised him a second visit in a short time, when she would reveal something of importance.

Rumours of when this ghost would appear with a mysterious message began to circulate and the consensus was that at midnight on Thursday the spirit would come to reveal all. Upwards of 1,000 people, a considerable amount for Sunderland's population at that time, showed up to see the amazing sight and congregated at a nearby churchyard in the hopes of catching a glimpse of the ghost travelling from its own narrow bed to that of the haunted man.

The crowd waited until 1 a.m. but their patience was not rewarded and no such event happened. Newspapers suggested that the spirit was merely taking a malicious pleasure in tantalising the poor mortals or that the crowd had simply got the day wrong. It was allegedly revealed the ghost had actually visited the man in the night on Wednesday, unfolding to him a tale of horror that it forbade him to reveal to any living person except the husband of his sister. The tale ends there but the question remains: why could the ghost itself not convey the message to her husband?

THE TYNE THEATRE

The theatre is a common setting for ghostly goings on, no matter where you visit. Perhaps this is down to how long they have existed or their proclivity to be a place of accidents before an age of health and safety. This short story tells of one such accident and a ghost that is said to remain in the Tyne Theatre.

Robert Crowther was employed at the theatre as a general worker with duties including setting and shifting scenes. One fateful night in April 1887, during the play *Nordisa*, he was hard at work when a frightful accident occurred. During the play, as was commonplace at the time, cannonballs were rolled along a surface to create the sound effect of thunder while the performance went on. One of these cannonballs got loose and landed on Robert's head, doing significant damage to his skull. Although he was rushed to the infirmary, the blow proved fatal and he sadly died only a few hours later. Over the years it is said there have been a few encounters with the ghost of the man who met his tragic end on a stage that still hosts so much even to this day.

THE SOUTH SHIELDS POLTERGEIST

While many ghost stories are often set many years in the past, here is an example of one from recent times. In 2006 on Lock Street in South Shields a couple and their young son, who wished to remain anonymous, began experiencing terrifying things going on in their family home. These included furniture being stacked on top of itself, doors and drawers opening, as well as objects being thrown across the room.

Paranormal Investigators Mike Hallowell and Darren Ritson were contacted and began to document what was happening at the property. In their book *The South Shields Poltergeist: One Family's Fight Against an Invisible Intruder*, the pair record the results of what they uncovered from the months spent investigating at the family's home. Physical attacks and apparitions are just some of the things they witnessed, with frequent activity taking place in their presence. One account from the book describes an encounter:

> The entity walked slowly from the bathroom, across the landing into the bedroom. As it passed Robert's room it paused and stared icily at me. Its face, devoid of all features such as eyes, nose or mouth, was cold and menacing. It felt like it was burrowing into my soul. It was large – maybe two meters in height – and midnight black. It was a three-dimensional silhouette that just radiated sheer evil.

The ordeal eventually came to a halt and there have not been any reports of major activity at the property since. If true, this is one of the most active and detailed recordings of a poltergeist to be shared with the public and it has taken place in a small town on our doorstep right here in South Shields.

THE CAULD LAD OF HYLTON

Perhaps Sunderland's most famous ghost story, this tale is believed to have taken place between the sixteenth and seventeenth centuries. Like many infamous local legends, there are different versions out there with minor details changing depending on who tells it, but the version described below holds many of the key details the majority have in common.

Robert Skelton was a young stable boy employed at the castle of Baron Hylton at the time these events are said to have taken place. Working in close proximity with the baron's daughter, the two began courting in secret due to their different status in society. When the baron found out he is said to have flown into a rage, murdering the stable boy with a pitchfork and dumping his body down a deep dark well. While the details often differ on the reasons, with some believing the boy was murdered because he did not prep his master's horse in time for an important journey, and also the varying method of his execution, the body is frequently described as having been disposed of down the well.

Several months later, the body was fished out from the well and the baron was put on trial for Robert's murder. He was acquitted thanks to an old farm hand providing an alibi. Soon after this, strange things began happening around the castle, such as chamber pots being emptied onto the floor and the kitchen being made a mess, despite having been tidied when everyone had gone to bed.

One dark night the cook stayed awake to catch the culprit, only to witness a naked boy crying out, 'I'm cauld!' The story goes that the cook and his wife left a cloak out for the wronged spirit, who promptly disappeared along with the disturbances although reports of the ghost continued well into the twentieth century.

This tale is a good example of how folklore can change and morph through the years, with different explanations and details and earlier versions stating that it was an elf or brownie that was the cause and not a ghost at all. While we may never know the exact origin of the story, records do show that Robert Hylton, the 13th Baron Hylton, was pardoned in 1609, suggesting there may be some truth to it after all.

LIFTING THE VEIL

In the early 1800s a woman named Martha Wilson was said to inhabit lodgings near the Newcastle Quayside. Distraught at having recently lost her beloved husband, she took her own life by hanging at her residence near Broad Chare.

She is often referred to as the 'Silky Ghost' and is said to have been spotted at a number of locations in the area. Her name is derived from the sound of her silk clothing rustling before she makes her appearance. One sighting describes how a local keelman, who is thought to have been aware of the stories, was walking home one night when he noticed someone following him on the other side of the road. Intrigued by this, he then began to follow the phantom through the crumbling streets to Trinity Chare. As he approached what he soon realised was a woman, she turned to him lifting her veil to reveal that she had no face, which sent the terrified man running in the opposite direction.

Due to her death being a suicide, Martha was denied a proper burial and her body was later found buried at a crossroads with a stake through her heart. Many believe that because of this her spirit cannot rest and she will continue to haunt those who are unlucky enough to cross her path.

GHOST SHIP

On 28 February 1855 the merchant vessel *Marathon*, of Newcastle upon Tyne, was south-west of the Azores when it happened to notice another ship sailing erratically. The *Marathon* made many attempts to hail the crew of the ship but received no response. As they pulled alongside, the curious crew began to notice strange details such as the rigging was tangled and the ship seemed in disorder, but most importantly there was no one at the wheel.

The seemingly abandoned ship was named the *James Chester*, sometimes referred to as the *James Cheston*, an American sailing ship. With a light breeze blowing, John B. Thomas, mate of the *Marathon*, lowered a boat and a party was sent aboard to investigate, the men likely already thinking of salvage rights. The ship was deserted with no crew present, but indications that something strange had happened could be seen. Furniture was said to be overturned, drawers ransacked and disorder could be found all over. Thoughts of piracy came to mind; however, much of the ship's cargo was still intact, and with no bloodstains or signs of violence this was ruled out. The question of what made these men abandon the vessel to risk their lives in the open sea no doubt worried the crew of the *Marathon*.

When Thomas later described his findings after his return to England more details came to light that are often left out of this story. The ship had taken on water through holes bored into its sides with a hatchet, but the amount was manageable as the pumps still functioned. The captain of the *Marathon* sent more men aboard and the *James Chester* was lightened enough that the ship could part with the *Marathon* and be brought to Liverpool, where it stood as a ghoulish curiosity.

Many versions of the story of this ghost ship have been told over the years, including links to giant octopus, the Bermuda Triangle and pirates. The reality of it, which is often left out, is that the crew of the *Chester* did reappear. Claims that no lifeboats were missing were incorrect, as a Dutch ship named *Two Friends* picked up some of the crew on 15 March. The captain of the ship, Joseph L. White, arrived in Delaware and conflicting stories as to why the ship was abandoned began circulating. Some said the ship was sinking and it was necessary while others accused the captain of intentionally attempting to sink the vessel. White and two of the ship's mates were arrested and the captain of the ghost ship was tried for unnecessarily abandoning the ship in an attempt to defraud insurance companies.

In an age before the internet, the story of this ghost ship has no doubt been told as non-fiction in a variety of different ways. It is an urban legend with little basis in truth that captured the minds of many. John B. Thomas of the *Marathon* was given great credit for rescuing the ship and bringing it to England, although little is known about the remainder of his life, as is the case with Captain White.

HAUNTED HOUSE

In February 1932, a story was published in the *Sunderland Echo* describing bizarre events taking place at a house in Sunderland on Northumberland Street. Following strange noises in the property, a spiritualist was drafted in and interviewed the deceased perpetrator, who had been causing the disturbance. During the interview the ghost gave the name of John Henry Turner and said he was wrongly convicted of a crime, which had led him to commit suicide. The spirit of John Turner also stated that he was earthbound and looking for someone named Annie so that his soul may rest in peace. The article stated: 'Almost every night between half-past eleven and midnight neighbours have heard mysterious noises on the stairs and knockings on the wall on the stair landing.'

The noises, which one man described as being similar to the noise of a man with a wooden leg walking up and down the stairs, had been occurring for a long time. Suspecting the noise could be coming from next door, the tenants asked the neighbours if they had been dusting their carpets at night, only to receive no satisfaction as to the explanation of the noise. Attempts to explain the situation even led the owners to think it might be cats, until one night when out in the yard the ghostly vision was witnessed in the form of a man wearing an overcoat.

They were not the only tenants to hear the sound, though, as a man who had previously lived there for twelve months corroborated their claim and said he was also unable to find an explanation for the noise.

Northumberland Street was eventually demolished as part of regeneration in the city. This begs the question of what happens to a ghost when the place he or she is haunting disappears?

THE HAUNTING OF WILLINGTON MILL

Willington Mill, built in 1800, was owned by two Quaker cousins named George Unthank and Joseph Procter, and was the first steam-powered mill in the North East. Rumours of spirits haunting the ground on which it was built can reportedly be traced back to the 1660s, when a woman who lived in a cottage there died and was buried in its grounds. In 1780, William Brown built a flour mill on the site of the cottage, which stood for twenty years before being demolished and replaced with the more modern Willington Mill.

Sometime between being built and 1806, two murders took place on the grounds, with neither victim being identified. In what would have been a small community at the time, these unexplained events would have no doubt created a lot of gossip. Another story tells how a woman got caught in a machine and was killed, leaving her spirit to haunt the mill. Joseph Proctor and his family moved into the property and began to experience strange things happening such as bizarre noises, apparitions and poltergeist-like activity.

This mill's reputation for being haunted spread and in 1840 a surgeon from Sunderland named Edward Drury, reportedly known for being a sceptic, was permitted to stay the night with his companion, Thomas

Hudson, a chemist from South Shields. The two men searched the house and, satisfied that no one was hiding or no tricks were being played, settled in for the night. Drury was later carried from the house screaming after hearing noises and seeing the ghostly apparition of a woman. He had no recollection of the previous three hours. In 1842, M.A. Richardson published *Authentic account of a visit to the haunted house at Willington*, which would later be republished in his book the *Local Historians Table Book*, which documents the unusual in the North East.

In 1890 the mill was closed and turned into a warehouse and the house turned into separate apartments. The high number of witnesses to these paranormal events made the haunting at Willington Mill notorious and even Sir Arthur Conan Doyle was said to acknowledge its credibility.

GHOSTS AND MISCHIEF

In February 1851 a great deal of excitement was caused in Boldon by what some believed to be a restless spirit. Numerous windows were smashed in one property and the spooky events caused so much trouble that one villager decided to stay awake to catch the culprit. An aged labourer armed with a blunderbuss agreed to keep watch in the hope of putting an end to the mischief. As the clock struck midnight, the man reported seeing the spirit of a black and white dog run between his legs, throwing him off his feet and setting the gun off. The following night three stalwart yeomen reported to be armed 'with firelocks and rum punch' kept guard but they too were terrified by what they believed to be the growl of a wild bear. Finally, having heard the sound of glass breaking, a police constable checked the property only to find a servant girl picking up rock fragments and throwing them at the window before running into the property and screaming, 'Mother, the ghost has come again'. The two women were brought before South Shields Magistrates for pretending to be ghosts but as no law existed to deal with ghosts they were discharged.

The next tale of spooky goings on took place at Hedworth Church. It was reported nationwide in 1896 that a great number of people had testified to seeing a ghost-like figure in the church window for more than a month. Rational explanation for the events could not be found and with people eager to find answers, a bounty was said to have been placed on the ghost. The alleged ghost sightings drew people from across the North East, all hoping to catch a glimpse of the shadowy figure. One member of the public theorised that the spirit looked like the late vicar who had died four years ago. It was stated that the spirit only appeared at the services on Sunday mornings and evenings; however, many were quick to point out that the ghost did not have a beard like the vicar he was said to resemble. Interestingly, one report points out that some people stated that just because someone had a beard in this life did not mean he would have one in the next. Despite having the church more full than it had been previously, the vicar at the time, Rev. E.S. Sykes, was said to be greatly annoyed by the commotion caused.

The sightings of the ghost at Hedworth Church died down and its presence was almost forgotten. That being said, two men in particular did not forget and were found in Boldon churchyard attempting to call forth the ghost. Matthew Stafford and Thomas McKenna were arrested on 2 October by PC Garbut, who was drawn to the churchyard by the shouts at 11.30 p.m. When the policeman reached the men they reportedly said they 'didn't care a __ for the ghost'. When asked what was the matter the men said they were looking for the spirit; however, it soon transpired the men had been drinking. Both Matthew and Thomas pleaded guilty to the charge of being drunk and disorderly and were ordered to pay a fine of 5s.

FIGHTING GHOSTS

Following the death of the landlord at the now long-gone Bull and Dog Tavern in Sunderland High Street, rumours began to circulate about spirits being seen in the building. Mr Barron, the landlord, died suddenly without a will, leaving property to the value of £16,000, which was to revert to the Crown. It was reported in the *Newcastle Guardian* and *Tyne Mercury* in January 1857 that: 'Several superstitious persons openly asserted they had seen the spectral shapes, and it was also stated the people of the house were afraid to live in it.'

A reward of £100, a considerable sum at the time, was offered to any two men who would stay in the house and guard them from the fearful apparition. It appears the reward was tempting enough for two brave lads from Hartley's Glass Works to offer to stay in the haunted house – however, for reasons unknown they were not admitted.

On Wednesday 21 January, as the sun was going down and leaving the city in near darkness, a crowd began to form in front of the pub. It is estimated no fewer than 3,000 people had gathered by 8 p.m. to watch the window of the house in the hope of catching sight of a visitor from beyond the grave. An hour or so later their wish was granted when two gigantic figures appeared in the window. Dressed in strange attire with one holding a battle axe and the other a sword, they began fighting before the stunned audience. When the swordsman thrust his weapon into the other ghostly figure, shrieks were let out from the shocked mass of people. The other figure armed with a battle axe brought his mighty weapon down on his foe before both characters vanished.

The terrified spectators remained staring at the window until past 11 p.m. in disbelief at what had just occurred before their very eyes. The following night another crowd began to form but this time the police stationed nearby moved the anxious audience along. It was then revealed that the ghouls the crowd had been watching were nothing more than officers from Oddfellows lodge who had been meeting in the building, and that the combat everybody had witnessed was nothing more than a practical joke performed by two of its members after the lodge had closed.

GHOST HUNTING

In 1901 reports began to surface of a house in Blaydon experiencing suspected paranormal activity. The property, occupied by an unnamed widow and her family, was being plagued with mysterious tapping that was without an explanation.

Offers to help with the ghostly problem came in and access to the property was granted. The group of ghost hunters scoured the alleged haunted house but were unable to solve the issue of the mystery noises. Assembling in the kitchen, where the source of the noise was believed to be, one of the group had the idea of removing a floorboard. To the surprise of all involved, a stampede of ghosts was found in the form of rats that had been living beneath the property.